ROADHOUSE BLUES

SE BLUES

MORRISON,
THE DOORS,
AND THE
DEATH DAYS
OF THE SIXTIES

BOB BATCHELOR

HAMILCAR
PUBLICATIONS
BOSTON

ISBN: 978-1949590-54-8

CIP data is available.

hamilcarpubs.com

Aut viam inveniam aut faciam

TO SUZETTE,
ALWAYS MY MUSE AND BEST FRIEND. ALL MY LOVE!

TO JEROME CHARYN,
FOR ENCOURAGEMENT AND FOR HELPING ME FIND MY MUSIC . . .

Jim Morrison was inspired by an array of poets, writers, and philosophers. Some of his influences were American writers, such as F. Scott Fitzgerald, William Faulkner, and Ernest Hemingway. One of his favorites was Norman Mailer, with whom Morrison shared a deeply questioning nature and a turn toward the dark aspects of the human condition, as in the singer's favorite novel, *The Deer Park* (1955). Jim drew from the Beat poets (Allen Ginsberg, Lawrence Ferlinghetti, and Michael McClure) and philosophers and writers Franz Kafka, Friedrich Nietzsche, and Vladimir Nabokov. Morrison owed a major intellectual debt to Arthur Rimbaud, whom he idolized as a poet and nineteenth-century mythmaker. In film, Jim looked to Jean-Luc Godard. He also drew inspiration from James Joyce and Louis-Ferdinand Céline. Musical influences included Bing Crosby, Frank Sinatra, Elvis Presley, and Bob Dylan.

Education

St. Petersburg Junior College

Florida State University

University of California, Los Angeles, B.A. 1965

BORN DECEMBER 8, 1943, MELBOURNE, FLORIDA

Morrison had two books of poems published in his lifetime. He had others published posthumously.

Death: July 3, 1971

James Douglas Morrison

Raymond Daniel Manzarek, Jr.

BORN FEBRUARY 12, 1939, IN CHICAGO (SOUTH SIDE)

Ray Manzarek was a classically trained blues-jazz keyboard player, but learned to play bass parts on the piano in a simplistic repetitive technique with his left hand, which produced the Doors' hallmark sound. His style grew from the music he heard obsessively listening to the radio as a kid on the South Side of Chicago: boogie-woogie piano and Chicago-based blues, played by Little Richard, Fats Domino, and Muddy Waters. His bass keyboard influences included Albert Ammons, Clarence "Pinetop" Smith, and Meade Lux Lewis. From jazz, Manzarek drew from the greats, including John Coltrane and Bill Evans. He also borrowed from the Latin-infused jazz popular in Southern California. Similar to Morrison, his intellectual debts ranged from the Beats to contemporary European filmmakers. He brought his film influences into the Doors' idea of creating musical theater; those influences ranged from Ingmar Bergman and Federico Fellini to Akira Kurosawa and Satyajit Ray.

Education

DePaul University, B.A. 1960

University of California, Los Angeles, M.F.A. 1965

Death: May 20, 2013

Robert Alan Krieger

BORN JANUARY 8, 1946, IN LOS ANGELES

Robby Krieger's early musical influences included Frank Sinatra, Elvis Presley, and Fats Domino. Krieger's parents were classical-music fans, so he listened to a lot of that particular genre growing up. Hearing Chuck Berry convinced him to play rock-and-roll guitar, but he was initially a classical player focusing on flamenco and jazz. Other jazz, blues, and rock guitarists who influenced him include Wes Montgomery, Robert Johnson, Albert King, and Larry Carlton. As a teenager, Krieger played in a jug band, a form popular in California at the time. Like many folk aficionados, he loved Bob Dylan, as well as the blues-laden and folk sounds of Koerner, Ray & Glover, and the Paul Butterfield Blues Band. He counts Joan Baez as another important musical figure. Later, he and John Densmore studied Indian music with Ravi Shankar.

Education

University of California, Santa Barbara

University of California, Los Angeles

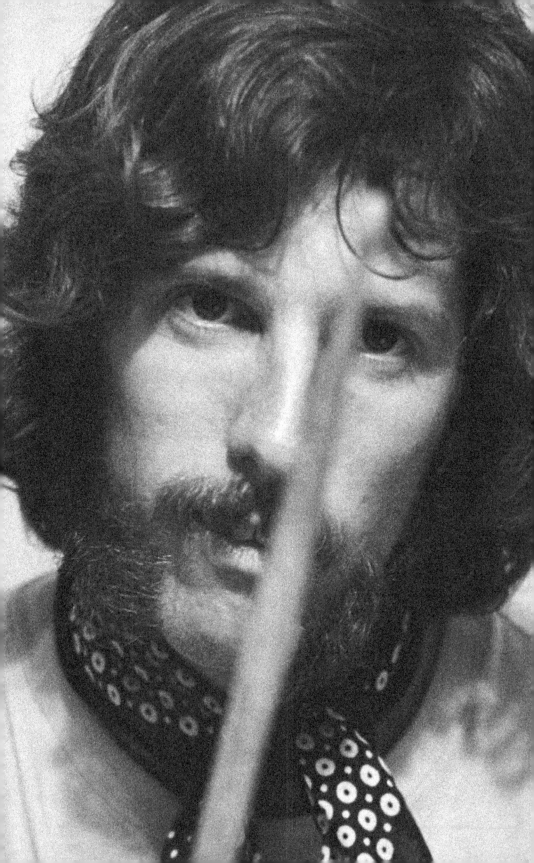

BORN DECEMBER 1, 1944, IN LOS ANGELES

Education

Santa Monica City College

California State University, Northridge

Originally a pianist who liked to improvise on classic and pop songs, **John Densmore** took up percussion in high school as a member of the band, which impacted his thinking on dynamics and the power of playing drums. His major influences came from jazz, including John Coltrane's drummer Elvin Jones and Art Blakey. Densmore also enjoyed Coltrane and Miles Davis. Densmore's use of bossa nova/samba, which had been developed in Brazil, was a driving force on many Doors songs.

John Paul Densmore

FOREWORD

Almost alone among the Flower Power acts along the Sunset Strip or down in Laurel Canyon, the Doors radiated menace. Only the band Love, fronted by the pugnacious Arthur Lee, could compete with Jim Morrison and Co. for atomizing the plastic veneer of a Los Angeles fantasia—that of a West Coast paradise awash in good vibrations.

As Bob Batchelor outlines in *Roadhouse Blues*, the short but explosive career of the Doors dovetailed almost seamlessly with the rise and fall of the pseudo-utopian Sixties. No matter what the Mamas and the Papas or Jackie De Shannon or the Beach Boys sang, the dark side of the hippie generation loomed like an eclipse and, for a few brief years, the Doors were there to chronicle the blackening sun. "Their sound thumped and thundered, reflecting their era and projecting it out to audiences that were unnerved by its energy," writes Batchelor. "Jim knew what people wanted. 'America was conceived in violence. Americans are attracted to violence,' he later explained. 'They attach themselves to processed violence, out of cans. They're TV-hypnotized . . . they're emotionally dead.' The attraction–revulsion theme centering on elemental forces of light, dark, love, hate, life, and death would have been impossible for most bands to implement, but the Doors were staking their future on that principle."

Even with such idiosyncratic talents as Brian Wilson, Sky Saxon, Captain Beefheart, Dino Valenti, and Arthur Lee as regional contemporaries, Jim Morrison stood out. In Morrison, the Doors had a frontman equal parts Lord Byron, Artaud, and Scott Walker. Inspired by a theater background (before he graduated from UCLA with a degree in cinematography) and the poetry of the Beats, Morrison brought a rare erudition to the mic stand and the lyric sheet.

It was Nietzsche and Rimbaud, however, who drove Morrison to live on the dangerous edge of things. From Nietzsche, Morrison seemed to draw a general way of life from *Zarathustra*: "One must have chaos in oneself to be able to give birth to a dancing star." From Rimbaud, Morrison borrowed much more, including the pre-Surrealist stylings for his verse and the destructive notion of altered states of mind amounting to enlightenment. "A poet makes himself a visionary," Rimbaud wrote, "through a long, boundless, and systematized disorganization of all the senses." Also like Rimbaud, who was often flea-bitten and adrift, Morrison adopted vagabondage as a modus vivendi. For the last five or six years of his life, Morrison had no fixed residence. Indeed, when he fortuitously ran into Ray Manzarek on Venice Beach in July 1965, he was essentially homeless. Dropping acid regularly, crashing with friends, reading dog-eared paperbacks, writing poetry with the booming Pacific waves as a soundtrack, Morrison straddled two overlapping eras (both soon to be bygone): the last decades to produce the bohemian litterateur and the hippie dropout as social types.

In *Roadhouse Blues*, Bob Batchelor chronicles the whirlwind rise and fall of the Doors and how their brief but riotous career paralleled the chaos of the 1960s. Batchelor, a cultural historian who has written about topics as diverse as *Mad Men*, the Prohibition bootlegger George Remus, and Marvel Comics super-impresario Stan Lee, turns his critical eye to the days when rock and roll (and particularly the Doors) was considered revolutionary. "The notion that music could transform society at the individual level and as a whole permeated the Sixties," writes Batchelor. "We might see this as trite today, but the idea felt alive then—palpable—and this gives context to how the Doors were formed and the philosophies they embraced."

Named after an Aldous Huxley memoir (which itself paraphrased William Blake) about a psychedelic experience, "The Doors," writes

Batchelor, "were nothing like the Beatles or the American rock bands that were starting to gain traction at the time."

Featuring a classically trained pianist playing basslines on a Fender Rhodes bass piano with his left hand and mesmerizing runs on a Vox Continental organ with his right, the Doors were unique from the beginning. Add a guitarist with training in flamenco and a drummer whose idol was Elvin Jones, and you have genuine originals, even during an era as experimental as the Sixties were. At times, the Doors sounded funereal, other times vibrant, still others carnivalesque, and, finally, they bordered on apocalyptic. The hellfire atmosphere the Doors radiated is best embodied by "The End," their epic phantasmagoria that culminates, lyrically, in family annihilation.

With his steady baritone, his gaunt good looks, his skintight leather pants, and his open defiance of all that was wholesome, Morrison became an unlikely sex symbol, even popping up in the pages of *Vogue* and *16* magazine. The disconnect between Morrison and the teenybopper set who read idealized portraits of the "Lizard King" in *16* led critics to turn against the Doors, especially after they released *The Soft Parade*, their fourth album, featuring brass horns, saxophones, and a string orchestra. To his detractors (Lester Bangs called him "Bozo Dionysus), Morrison was a pretentious phony, cribbing from the Living Theater, Brecht, and the Beatniks of the 1950s.

This critique fails on two levels: first, Morrison lived his ideals (no matter how much those ideals were anathema to the armchair set). Like some of his peers, David Crosby, Grace Slick, and Gram Parsons, Morrison abandoned a comfortable upbringing to pursue his personal vision; and when he died in 1971, at the age of twenty-seven, his conscious pursuit of oblivion could hardly be considered insincere. Second, precious few pop acts were infusing their work with avant-garde influences, and to consider that a drawback seems almost parochial.

But critics were not the only ones who eyed the Doors and Morrison suspiciously. To what has been popularly known as "The Establishment," Morrison was a moving target, with his own FBI file and a series of run-ins with law enforcement based on his amoral pursuit of hedonism and his potential as some sort of revolutionary spark plug. For the love generation, it was business as usual. "The rock-and-roll lifestyle came under fire when tied so closely to drug use, rebellion, and anarchy," writes Batchelor.

"The Rolling Stones were pitched to the world as the anti-Beatles, a group of young hellions who epitomized the wild side. Their mix of loud rock music tinged with rhythm and blues—another trait shared with the Doors—provided the soundtrack for the global counterculture. For those in power, however, their revolution had to be quelled."

Today it seems almost inconceivable that the lead singer of one of the biggest pop acts in America could be maced by police before a concert, then pummeled after the show and dragged off to jail. But Morrison so embodied the counterculture—and all its nihilism—that his celebrity status offered no immunity from stormtrooper tactics. If anything, his stature as a leather-clad rabble-rouser only made him more of a mark for law-and-order zealots.

In 1969, Morrison, the self-styled shaman/showman, no longer enamored with fame but still drinking and abusing drugs, was hurtling toward self-destruction when he was charged with lewd and lascivious behavior, indecent exposure, profanity, and drunkenness stemming from a shambolic concert in Miami. His subsequent trial and conviction effectively ended the Doors as a live act and left Morrison contemplating poetry and film as alternatives to music. He would never get the chance to reinvent himself.

If the Doors were not the embodiment of revolution during the Age of Aquarius, they were certainly prophets of its failure. In *Roadhouse Blues*, Bob Batchelor contextualizes the Doors phenomenon with verve and a solid understanding of the electrifying and often contradictory Sixties.

Carlos Acevedo
New York City
September 2022

CONTENTS

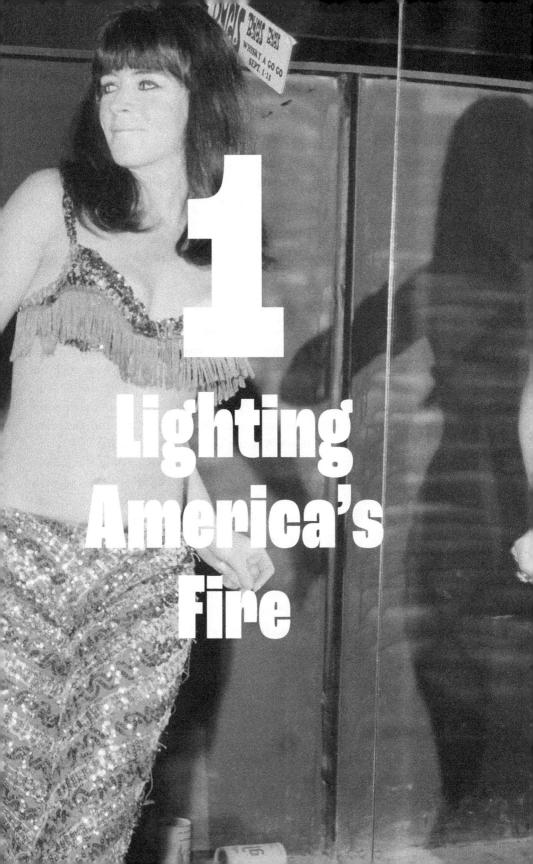

1
Lighting America's Fire

Light My Fire" hit its stride as the song tumbled toward the end. It seemed as if all of America had heard Ray Manzarek's carnivalesque organ when the song rocketed to number one months earlier. As Manzarek played, Robby Krieger churned out chords and fell into rhythm behind him. John Densmore pushed the beat with an intensity that belied his smooth demeanor. The sound was instantly recognizable and unlike anything rock fans had ever heard. They knew it by heart after hearing it on constant rotation all summer long.

In January when the record hit stores, no one would have anticipated that a moody, psychedelic single by an unheralded band would soon top the charts.

Now, here they were—*The Ed Sullivan Show*, their first national television appearance.

Jim Morrison growled out the last "Fi-ya-ah-ahh," then looked heavenward. He raised the microphone to his mouth and faced the camera in profile—prolific, Adonis—the shaggy hair, the cheekbones beaming out at America. As Densmore bashed the drums behind him, the leather-clad singer puffed out his chest at an angle and cocked his head the opposite way. He dropped his right arm alongside his thin frame and kicked his hips left. The crafted pose of America's latest teen heartthrob.

For millions of families gathered together across the nation, the *Sullivan Show* was a Sunday night tradition. Morrison's midriff appeared squarely in the middle of the screen as the camera moved in for a close-up. His well-worn white shirt with frayed cuffs peeked out from the black leather jacket, which contrasted against the gaudy red stage backdrop of actual doors hanging from the walls with Day-Glo yellow accents. Imagine the thoughts running through the mind of the countless American dads who had grown up listening to big bands like Benny Goodman and Glenn Miller. They glanced up at the TV set, the cacophony drawing their attention for just a moment. Quickly, their eyes dialed in on the spectacle.

Jim's leather pants were slung low on his waist. Something else was prominently on display—practically unavoidable. What could these dads have thought, how did they see that moment?

As Ray's organ grinded on—mesmerizing—the camera zoomed out. Morrison stood stoically, not looking up. Then, twirling the microphone in his outstretched fingers, he straightened and flung the chord over his shoulder, as if holding a quiver of arrows. Then, in a heartbeat, he smashed down, using the mic to hit the last note as the audience's first wave of shrieks struck the band. The teenage girls who filled the auditorium seats that night were ignited by the hit single and the chance to see the beautiful rock god in real life.

As the applause and screams grew louder, the singer finally recognized what had just happened. He drew them in, then looked up—vulnerable. Feeling the power of the moment, Jim bared his teeth, something between a snarl and a smile. He let out a little breath and stepped toward Sullivan. When the camera cut to the host, he clapped and mouthed something like "good job" toward Morrison, even though he must have already determined that the Doors would be banned forever from his show for using the lyrics "girl we couldn't get much higher." The show's producer had asked them to change it following that afternoon's sound check. Ed thought they all agreed that they would abide the decision.

Recalling that evening, Krieger wrote in his memoir that the guys were nervous doing Sullivan for the first time, perhaps no one more than Jim. He didn't like these appearances, sensing an inauthenticity in performing in the middle of day with the hot television lights beating down and everything so unnaturally bright.

Morrison liked a darker world. On tour, the singer frequently asked for the lights to be lowered at shows, especially in larger venues. Mood meant something to him. He preferred the dingy clubs where the band had developed their sound since forming just a little more than two years earlier. He also liked to have a couple of drinks to set the tone for the evening.

Television, on the other hand, made Morrison edgy and self-conscious (though no one could have imagined Jim lacking confidence based on the performance that he had just delivered). Rather than Jim making some artistic point by sticking to the original lyrics, Krieger thought that he simply forgot to change them as requested, most likely too caught up in the moment—or maybe he wasn't even paying attention when Sullivan's producer asked him to.

We'll never know the full truth, but it's problematic to attribute the mistake to anxiety. Jim's anti-authority streak was too strong. He loathed anyone who had the audacity to tell him what to do. When pushed, Morrison rammed back harder. What could they do to him if he didn't sing the other phrase? If this were gasoline, Jim was willing to pull out his matches.

The Doors performed on the *Ed Sullivan Show* on September 17, 1967—just three years after the Beatles transformed the music business and American culture. They had almost single-handedly revolutionized music and distracted the nation from the tragedy of John F. Kennedy's assassination. Other guests who shared the bill with the Doors that night included actor Yul Brynner and rising comedian Rodney Dangerfield.

But it was the Doors and Morrison they wanted. Scores of teenyboppers waited in line on 54th Street to get a seat. Backstage, Ed mingled with the guests in the dressing rooms, but it was his son-in-law Bob Precht who served as producer of the collective cacophony that was America's most beloved variety show.

After getting through sound check, Precht met up with the band backstage. "You boys look great when you smile," he supposedly told them, adding, "Don't be so serious." Of course a world-class wiseass like Jim couldn't let that slide. "Well, uh, we're kind of a sullen group," he allegedly told the producer.

Morrison and his bandmates had worked hard to perfect that moody, glowering aura. This was Jim's zone, the place where he could turn on and off different personas depending on his frame of mind and the crowd's reaction to the music. The Doors projected darkness. Fans would follow them, either to live out their own fantasies through Morrison or to hold the group up as antiheroes in a mostly generic pop-music world. The Doors were nothing like the Beatles or the American rock bands that were starting to gain traction at the time. Although on paper they were just four young guys in a rock group, they exuded a certain dangerousness.

Why did this matter as they prepared to go on the Sullivan show? In short, there was no way the Doors or Morrison were going to go on national television and pretend to be smiley or cheerful. That wasn't their gig.

As if the "smile" comment wasn't enough, Precht was the one who had told the band that Morrison couldn't sing the lyrics "much higher" on national television. Despite teenagers and other young men dying in the jungles of Vietnam and civil rights activists being brutalized in the American South, the producer feared that TV viewers might interpret the lyrics (correctly) as a drug reference.

Speaking for the entire band, Ray told Precht they would alter the lyrics. The decision dropped a cloud over the pre-show festivities, which up to that point had been fun, as the guys clowned around together to allay some jitters. Ray, Robby, and John weren't really sure what Jim would do when the cameras rolled. Knowing the singer, though, they had a hunch he wouldn't comply. Densmore remembered Jim's reaction as "rage" and that Morrison represented "a possible explosion too near the surface to mess with."

Years later Robby recalled the episode differently, portraying the band as defiant and unified in the face of the producer's demand: "We thought they were joking . . . wanting us to change the lyrics on the number-one song in America? We decided to just do the song as-is . . . we didn't care."

What did America see that night? They may not have realized it, but it was the rise of a new spirit emanating from the West. The Doors would take the influences of the West Coast—psychedelics, jam-band techniques, free love, peace, activism, and a concern for life and the larger world—and deliver it to the nation. California, according to one journalist, was the land of culture and "thinking man's society." As a result, "About 75 percent of the groups hitting today call somewhere in California their home."

Jim was even more direct, explaining, "The path of the sun leads to the West. There's a new life out there. New York is decaying. The West is vibrant and strong." Ray echoed his sentiment, noting the "vitality" of their adopted home. In an interview he said, "You feel closer to the earth when the weather is always warmer and you can be sunk in seawater up to your nose twenty minutes from home."

Although the song "The End" became a crowd favorite—and infamous—based on its Oedipal overtones and foreboding essence, the last line is literally a command. Jim urged the listener to get to California.

After the declaration, "The West is the best," he admonished: "Get here and we'll do the rest!" Los Angeles, Morrison's adopted home, could be considered the end of the nation, but what he meant by "the rest" is unclear. If nothing else, "The End" is the first in a series of love letters he would write to the City of Lights that exposed its mystery, allure, and seedy underbelly. Danger lurked there with Jim as the devil-on-the-shoulder guide to LA's charms and decadence.

The West as America's cure-all and future had long been a part of the national character. But the region was still misunderstood and constantly in flux. While much of the nation might have viewed the West through the lens of cowboys and ranchers, like on the hit TV shows *Gunsmoke* and *Bonanza*, the real West had a long history of jumbling together different people, cultures, and experiences, like the Native Americans who settled the region and the Spanish people who explored it and set up a network of missions up and down the coast. Yet *Bonanza* was the number-one-rated show on television in 1967, the same time the Doors exploded onto the scene with "Light My Fire." How did Middle America rectify these unrelated images—one the exemplar of the new youth culture, the other Hollywood's repackaging of a mythic and mostly inaccurate past?

A more accurate model for the changing West was probably the 1965 Watts Riots, when a botched drunk-driving arrest unleashed a week of mayhem and death on Los Angeles. Over a six-day period in August, thirty-four people died, more than a thousand were injured, and four thousand were arrested.

The riots were sparked when Lee Minikus, a white California Highway Patrol officer, pulled over a car for allegedly driving recklessly in the Watts neighborhood of Los Angeles. Marquette Frye drove the vehicle. His step-brother Ronald occupied the passenger seat. Suspecting that Frye was drunk, Minikus had him perform a roadside sobriety test, which he failed. Arrested for drunk driving, Frye lashed out and a fight ensued. More cops arrived on the scene, as well as a crowd, including the driver's mother Rena, who lived just down the street. As the melee grew, other officers brandished shotguns and riot batons.

Confusion ruled as the situation escalated, fueled by a growing crowd of angry onlookers who mistrusted the police and saw their actions as abusive. Soon, hundreds of people gathered, as did dozens of cops. The scene ignited when the police attempted to arrest a woman—who looked to be pregnant—for spitting on them. Word quickly spread that officers had kicked a pregnant woman while she lay on the ground.

The situation rapidly deteriorated, resulting in crowds armed with bricks, rocks, and bottles facing off against the police. That evening, more people were drawn into the battle as stopped cars, drivers, and passengers (many white) were assaulted in protest of the earlier arrests. When darkness engulfed LA, clashes between the police and rioters resulted in buildings being set on fire and mass looting.

With the police overwhelmed, fourteen thousand National Guard troops entered the city and walled off sections with barricades in an attempt to bring order. There were reports of sniper fire and rioters throwing Molotov cocktails. The violent clashes continued, fanned by racist remarks made by the LA Police Commissioner.

When order was restored, observers noted that the police and National Guard response was brutal. Although a later investigation recommended new measures to create a safer, more-just environment in Watts, the suggestions were largely (and perhaps inevitably in that era) ignored.

For conservative America, the Watts uprising and brutal retaliation sent spasms of fear into the heartland. Yet the incident could be viewed as just a more egregious representation of the gulf between Black and white communities in the early and mid-1960s. Tensions between the police and those in Black neighborhoods created a wedge between people and punctuated the central role race would play in the decade and beyond.

For readers today, these scenes will of course ring true. It is as if the Sixties were replayed for an already tense nation with the murder of George Floyd and others by overzealous police officers. But the forces of evil simply had too much power in that earlier period. No Black Lives Matter type of response would have been tolerated.

The idea of setting the night on fire in the Doors' hit single created a symbolic moment that conjured the Watts Riot and others across the nation between 1960 and 1967. Young people who bought Doors records were often the same ones attuned to the atrocities plaguing American society.

As a representation of both California and a new spirit of unity, the Doors captured a sound that let in hope, rage, anarchy, and light.

According to jazz writer Michael Cuscuna, the band's eponymous debut album was "the first successful synthesis of jazz and rock . . . equally rooted in the spirit of rock and the feeling of jazz."

On top of that, Morrison heard Frank Sinatra and Elvis Presley in his head and had visions of Bob Dylan and the Beatles. When he wrote poems as songs and songs as poems, the concert unfurled in his mind's eye. Ray Manzarek's genius was rooted in two things: recognizing Morrison's star quality—something he had keyed in on since their days together at UCLA—and how he used Chicago jazz and blues to create a new kind of rock music.

While the issue of race didn't provide the main source of fuel for Jim, he had grown up in the South and understood its significance. The California twist was Morrison's experimentation with drugs, as he attempted to expand his mind like his literary heroes, the Beats, Jack Kerouac, and transgressive French poet Arthur Rimbaud. And his isolation and loneliness fed his poems and lyrics.

Like so many people in LA (then and since), Morrison also underwent a physical transformation. The lonely summer on a Santa Monica rooftop had re-created him physically. Always labeled "chubby," he dropped 35 pounds and weighed around 130 pounds. Gaunt looked good on Jim. He transformed from a silly dilettante at UCLA—one not even that popular among his fellow kooks and misfits—into a bohemian male model. His hair grew out and framed his now-angular features. His paunchy midriff became sculpted. Morrison learned how to manipulate his body. He practiced in front of mirrors, crowds, and on stage and slowly grew into the persona that reflected full-blown transformation.

Jim's singing voice was the final component. Although diffident, he began imagining himself as a rock star. That fateful day on the beach when Ray boasted that they should form a band and make a million dollars? Jim's response: "That's what I wanted all along."

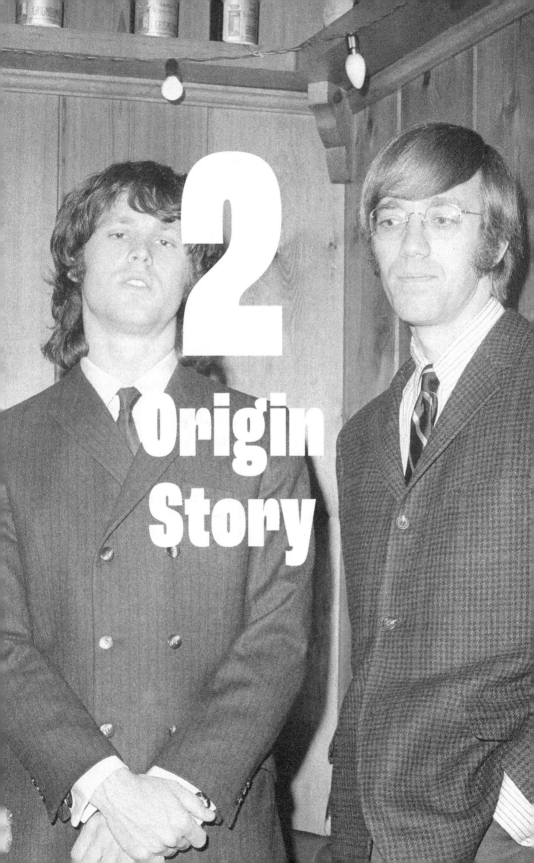

2
Origin
Story

Many great bands from rock and roll's glory days have an origin story that is almost fanciful when retold later. Yet they all seem to begin at the same place—basically a couple of young guys bump into one another in an odd setting and start talking about music. Their enthusiasm whips into a crescendo that leads them to form a band. The rest is history.

One of the best examples is when former primary-school classmates Mick Jagger and Keith Richards ran into each at the Dartford train station in October 1961. They talked about the stack of imported rhythm and blues albums Mick was toting around. The mutual interest in R&B they discovered that day eventually launched the Rolling Stones.

There is often more than a touch of the apocryphal in many band-origin stories. Some are embellished; others are invented outright. In the early years of rock music, concocted stories helped sell a band to eager fans, reluctant music executives, and jaded music critics and journalists.

For an origin story to become truly memorable, it has to be short—so that it can be told fairly quickly—and it has to have some interesting hook that makes the event seem almost divinely predestined. What sets these moments in time apart from *normal* life? There must be the thunderbolt moment when the idea crystallizes. Hardwired genetically and culturally to understand the world through stories, people opt into the twist-of-fate story line. The fantastical element leaves people later asking: "Did this really happen so innocently?" At the heart of the story is the notion that if the life-changing moment could happen to them, well, then it could happen to/for me too.

The Doors story begins with Jim Morrison and Ray Manzarek haphazardly running into each other on Venice Beach. The two college friends—both adrift in the postcollege world with little clue what to do next—catch up on their lives over the last couple months.

In Manzarek's retelling, they almost immediately hit on their shared interest in music—in dialogue that sounds like Sixties Stereotypes 101:

It was a beautiful California day in July around one in the afternoon, when who comes walking down the beach but James Douglas Morrison. And I said, "Hey, man, what have you been doing? How come you're still here in LA?"

Rather than reply truthfully: "Living on a rooftop—taking a lot of acid," Jim explains that "he was writing some songs."

A consummate musician and veteran of several bands, Ray goaded his hesitant friend into singing one of his tunes. Jim meekly launches into "Moonlight Drive," instantly winning over Manzarek with the haunting lyrics. Perhaps more important, Ray heard potential.

Looking back on that moment—though he wasn't there—Robby Krieger echoed Ray: "Those first songs he came up with, he actually heard them in his head. It was like a concert being played in his head." Similarly, John Densmore recounted what Jim had told him about his early songwriting attempts: "He said to me that he thought of melodies to remember the words . . . that's really a gift."

I like counterfactual history—which is examining a piece of history that happened and imagining either that it didn't take place or that it may have unfolded in ways that we haven't considered. In other words, it is the great "what if" moment that illuminates our perspective by thinking about a person, place, thing, or episode from new points of view. The value in reconsidering is that it lights avenues that may have been shut off, especially when mulling over things that hinge on anecdote, hearsay, or people's memories.

With the Doors, we're asking, "Is this what happened or does the story transform in the moment or over time?" If so, what does it mean about the person telling it and the way people engage with storytelling? For example, in an interview with journalist Bob Micklin at the end of 1967, Manzarek said, "I happened to run into Jim on the beach." This clarification counters the traditional origin story that has the young lion wandering through the sand and stumbling upon Ray. This is a minor blip in the retelling, but critical if we want to come to a fuller meaning. (By the way, Oliver Stone's film *The Doors* also has Jim walking down the beach—wearing a black T-shirt thereby providing a mind's-eye perspective for fans less steeped in those early moments.)

However, let's look at an even more interesting counterfactual. What if Jim knew that Ray would be at the beach? How does it transform our perception if we consider that Morrison purposely searched Manzarek out? He could have been lonely or perhaps hoping to get feedback on his lyrics from an established musician.

If we look at the sweep of events from Jim's standpoint, he was essentially homeless and didn't have much money. He'd written off his parents—his source of income and support—and didn't leave for New York City as he had planned and discussed with Ray after graduation. Instead, via prolific amounts of LSD (still legal at the time), he found his consciousness expanded. He heard concerts in his mind and his poems burst to life as lyrics. Perhaps most amazingly, he remembered both the words and melodies when the drugs wore off.

When Jim began viewing his poems as songs, he made an almost unthinkable leap to imagining himself as a singer, even though his only previous attempts were horsing around with Ray's band in and around UCLA.

In this alternative scenario, as one of his closest college friends, Ray might then serve as the conduit to the dreams of concerts that danced through his head. So, in response, Jim trudges toward Ray's place on the beach. He's not sure of what he'll say when he gets there, but he has to have someone else hear the songs that are on a continuous loop in his mind. Instead of knocking on Manzarek's door, Jim stumbles into him on the beach as he is on his own mental journey—listening to the waves and trying to figure out what his future holds.

In other words, Ray is receptive to what Jim is proposing in the moment. And rather than laughing in his friend's face or blowing him off because he's never sung before at any level, Manzarek gives him attention and encouragement. At the time, Ray may have felt generally purposeless, but he was the bandleader of a fairly successful local group that had scored countless gigs and a small-time recording contract. How many professional musicians would give a wannabe vocalist the time of day in this situation, even if they were friends? No one would commit to someone that raw unless he saw something exceptional.

Flashing back to the origin story, we might now view it as a series of smart moves that came from the serendipitous encounter. Together the two determine that Jim's lyrics are haunting and fantastic, then Ray hears how he would craft them into songs on the organ, and they decide to form a band. Going by the official, band-sanctioned timeline, the two young men have made some momentous decisions in a rather short amount of time. Then, as if it hasn't been laid out perfectly to this point, they promptly agree on Jim's name for the group (determining they couldn't continue as Rick & the Ravens). Finally, they peg their hopes, dreams, and aspirations to an outlandish objective: "make records and a million dollars."

The Doors as a moneymaking venture has been widely left out of the official record. If we are going to take the surviving Doors at their word, though, then the declaration tying their music to their financial aspirations needs to be counted too. In some instances Ray would later say that the "million dollars" part of the story was said tongue-in-cheek, but regardless it is a point of interest for anyone digging into the band's story.

So what matters most when we look back? Is it important to know who was walking down the beach or who said what? Could Ray and Jim—in the many hours they spent writing, composing, and talking about their new band—have made up the entire story (or at least rounded out its edges) as they dreamed of fame and fortune? Tactically, if a guy with a master's degree and his college-grad buddy are trying to become famous, one can imagine them being strategic enough to create a compelling origin story to help sell themselves to fans, journalists, and record executives.

Any questions that could be raised about the innocence of that fateful meeting center primarily on the blurry line between art and commerce. Ray also had an advanced degree in the Los Angeles music scene and understood the challenges confronting any band that hoped to get a record deal, let alone with an untested singer. His lightning-bolt, genius moment was recognizing the latent talent before him. Densmore shared this perspective, explaining, "The extremely important thing to know is that Ray was the first to see the magic in Jim Morrison." Manzarek understood his deeply philosophical and intellectual friend well enough to guide him to a shared vision.

Over the next several years, Ray and Jim would be reborn. The Doors would become a reality, and their lives would change forever. Working on their sound, they closely watched what other bands did to achieve success, and, like everyone in the mid-1960s, they watched how the Beatles, Rolling Stones, and Bob Dylan created personas to sell records and reach the rock-and-roll dream.

When Ray and Jim decided to start a band, the hurdle was that Manzarek already had a band—Rick & the Ravens—with his brothers Jim and Rick.

Morrison had seen the group play many times at UCLA, and even joined them on stage occasionally. Once, when the band played a gig and one of the members couldn't show, they paid Jim twenty-five bucks to stand there and pretend to play an unplugged electric guitar. Known for rousing, good-time songs, like "Louie Louie" and "Hoochie Coochie Man," Rick & the Ravens were popular enough to score a minor record deal with Aura Records.

After months of rehearsal—including drummer John Densmore joining the group in August—and shaping both Morrison's songs and voice, the Doors recorded a six-song demo in early September 1965. (All six, including the standards "Hello, I Love You" and "Moonlight Drive," would eventually be re-recorded by the band.)

With a sample in hand, the group did all they could to get it listened to by area record execs and producers. The reaction was tepid, to say the least. The Manzarek brothers were so disgusted by the rejection that they quit the band. They never really got Morrison's songs anyway. Rather than disband, however, Jim and Ray doubled down, searching immediately for a guitarist to fill the void. When Robby Krieger—Densmore's friend and former bandmate in the Psychedelic Rangers—joined in October, the Doors were complete.

Part of the challenge for record labels was that the Doors didn't look or sound like other bands—there was no one to compare them to. They pitched the demo to Columbia Records producer Billy James after seeing his beard in a photo. They figured he was a hip guy and might appreciate the raw edge of the record. According to James, "[They] had a quality that attracted me to them immediately." He also liked that Jim and Ray were college grads, thinking, "here are some intellectual types getting involved with rock and roll." After listening to them, he recognized that the Doors were "unlike anything I was familiar with." The producer also noticed the lyrics.

James signed the band to a five-and-a-half-year contract with a six-month initial deadline that required them to cut a series of singles in that first part of the deal. Jim, Ray, Robby, and John were ecstatic but realized that they would have to work even harder to sharpen their sound for Columbia—the home of Dylan and so many other greats. They used the record deal to try to score some gigs but were typically relegated to small-time shows where they played mostly cover songs and tried to insert a couple of originals.

What the Doors did right—like the Beatles and Stones had done at the early stages of their careers—was put in the work that helped them mesh as a band. They also made important decisions about sharing credit for writing and publishing as a group—rather than individually—and determined that all critical matters would be resolved by unanimous vote. The Doors functioned as a collective, not only musically but as a business.

The record deal was a significant milestone, but creating a sound was the true goal. Elektra founder Jac Holzman, who would soon play a decisive role in the band's trajectory, identified some of the factors that helped them chart the best course. From his perspective, it was Ray who had a vision of what the band could become:

> The thinking one in terms of conceptualizing and taking it all someplace was Ray. He had a sense from the very beginning of what it was that they had, of who Morrison was, of how to put it together, and I think he was a very special kind of glue that held it together. Every time Jim would go off on a tear it was Ray who made the band continue to happen.

Manzarek's leadership can't be overstated. Not only did he conceive of and launch the Doors' musical direction, but, more critically, he knew he had the right personalities. Ray sensed traits in John and Robby that he knew would work for the collective, just as he recognized the magic Jim brought to the band.

With Densmore, Ray leaned on his dedication to exploration and honing his art. John could be fiery and dramatic at times, but Manzarek knew he also wanted to fit in, to belong. John had the skill to be a Keith Moon–type drummer (one prone to big flourishes who tries to steal the spotlight from the singer), but he viewed himself in the tradition of great jazz players—you get your solo, but success was achieved collectively.

Robby Krieger, according to Holzman, "surfed whatever the wave of the Doors was." What Ray understood at Robby's audition was that despite being the youngest member, he was arguably the group's most gifted musician. His virtuosity immediately gave the band power and flexibility. Krieger was also the personification of *California cool*. His laid-back attitude counterbalanced Jim's unfailing oddness.

But Robby also had a more assertive and self-assured side. His initial assessment of the band and its front man was instructive. "Jim didn't make much of an impression on me when I first met him," Krieger remembered. Back then, Morrison was far removed from the wild stage persona he would later adopt. "He wore muted, drab clothes," the guitarist said. Far from seeing Morrison as a future rock star, Robby saw him as a quiet person with limited potential. He didn't even like the band name (unlike Ray and Jim who felt it perfectly encapsulated what they wanted to be and convey to the world). In early 2022, Krieger told a journalist: "I thought it was a dumb name. I didn't get it."

John may have shared Robby's initial ideas about the singer and the band's name, but he still wanted to get the guitarist to join the band. What can we say about Jim on the day of that fateful meeting? We know that he was typically a quiet person, and certainly so around strangers. Plus, Densmore introduced them in a location far removed from the wilds of Hollywood—Krieger's parents' home in the suburbs. "I figured it might be worth a shot," Robby said about joining the group.

The deal with Billy James—who had worked with Bob Dylan—was enough to commit Krieger to the project. Two of Jim's songs, "Moonlight Drive" and "End of the Night," convinced him that this band might have the right edge. As he recalled in his 2021 memoir, Morrison's lyrics "rattled around in my head long after Jim and John left my house."

Robby's decision to join the Doors remains a pivotal moment in rock history. Over the decades, Krieger has often been viewed as the Ringo of the band—the youngest and most compliant member vis-à-vis the stronger personalities of Morrison and the father figure Manzarek. But this perspective overlooks Robby's essential role in creating the band's sound. A virtuoso, he would later produce music so distinctive that on first listen you knew this could only be Robby Krieger.

While Morrison at the time was anxious, acid-addled, and looking for a persona that fit his new ambition, Krieger seemed to enter the group more fully formed as a human, despite his age. Although he got into a jam experimenting with marijuana—which got him sent to a private school in Menlo—he came from a prosperous, loving family. When he discovered the guitar, his dedication to learning the craft took over. Krieger mastered several styles, producing a sound that fit with Manzarek's vision but didn't simply slip into the keyboardist's approach. Instead, he created his own groove that would define the young band.

Looking at photos from the band's earliest days, taken during breaks from exhaustive practicing and bonding at Ray's beach pad, Jim does not look like the "young lion" from the now-ubiquitous portraits everyone recognizes or the leather-clad Lizard King (a nickname and persona Morrison created to transform from poet to rock icon). In fact, he looks frail and has long hair for the era but not the bushy mane he would make famous. Just a kid who looks like he could use a meal. So this begs the question: What did Ray see in this skinny kid who had big dreams but had never actually sung before?

From the moment he and Jim decided to form a band, Manzarek spent the rest of his life talking about the Doors and Morrison. He made their combined future seem predestined—that day on the beach led to eventual immortality. In the moment and in reality, however, Ray was taking a big gamble on a young man the rest of the world had basically given up on—after he drifted away from UCLA, Morrison began living with friends and on Santa Monica rooftops and no one expected much from him or for him to ever have a "real" job. In essence, he had little to offer except what he secretly valued most—his words and his voice.

There are some people who when they meet feel they have met before or sense a kind of kismet. If it's in a romantic sense, we often call this love at first sight. With Ray and Jim, it was a type of brotherly, spiritual bond that served each person's need. Ray needed to be the big brother/father figure, putting bands together, filmmaking, creating music, and hanging the sound on the organ, making him the de facto bandleader. Although Jim would occasionally assert his independence by rebelling against Ray, he yearned for someone to support him, someone to provide a handrail for the young man as he explored the ideas exploding in his head.

Throughout the ages, societies have built infrastructures to harness, yoke, or chain those who refuse to (or cannot) fit into their norms. What has changed in recent eras is that we look at this group differently based on new scientific and medical innovations, as well as shifts in culture.

What is safe to say in today's parlance is that Morrison was a person with neurodiversity, which led him to be perceived in ways that were misunderstood in his lifetime. With Ray's corroboration and collaboration, Jim could marry his vision of himself as a poet and an intellectual to the energy and work necessary to become a rock-and-roll star. What Manzarek did differently from other individuals and institutions in Morrison's life was to provide the emotional bond that Jim needed to anchor himself—as well as he could—to the dream of the Doors.

"It's funny, but it sounds like a bad movie script," Ray admitted about his unlikely encounter with Jim that summer. Two years later, recalling his reaction after Jim timidly delivered "Moonlight Drive," Manzarek thought to himself: "that was it."

"We said, 'Hey, we ought to form a group, and make records, and a million dollars,'" Manzarek remembered.

After "Light My Fire" hit number one on the singles chart and was the summer song of 1967, his prediction came true.

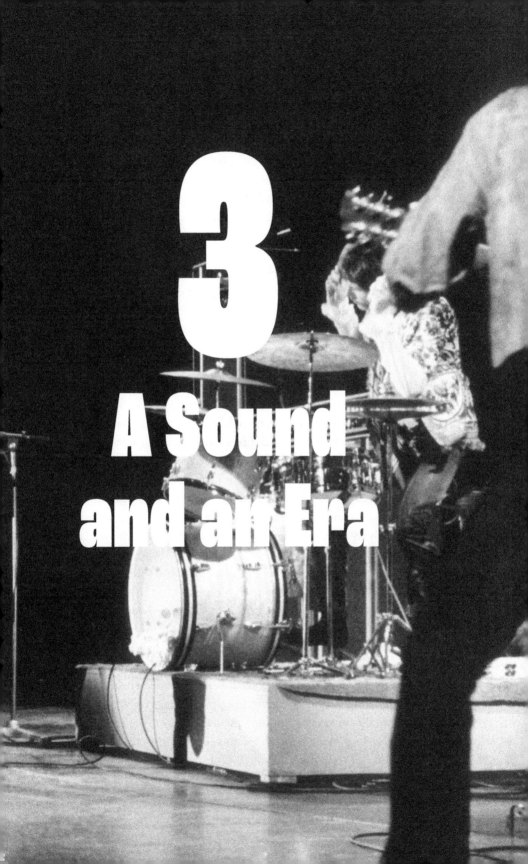

3

A Sound
and an Era

The persistence of the Sixties in people's minds centers on the eruption of political and social protest that marked the decade—the Civil Rights Movement, women's rights activism, and the antiwar movement. Across the era, young people found a cause to either yearn for or battle against. Looking back many decades later, the most enduring images of the era are of protests and violence.

Of course, Sixties "counterculture" included much more than these specific "issue-oriented" movements. It extended to more "lifestyle-oriented" movements as a variety of groups—most of which came to be labeled under the rubric of "hippies"—sought alternative ways of living that shunned the aggressive, money-driven world of capitalism.

It's difficult to imagine today why the parents, authority figures, and institutions of the Sixties had such a hard time accepting that young people wanted change. Did these movements threaten the so-called "American Way of Life"?

Fear certainly played a key role in the backlash against activism—fear of chaos, fear of drugs, fear of losing economic status, and more—let alone the existential fear of the Red Menace at the heart of the Cold War. While the average citizen could never confront Russia, they could easily rail against hippies. And this reactionary intensity toward a deviant lifestyle only increased because of young people's drug use. And since rock bands provided a rallying point for teenagers and young adults, they became an easy target for conservative groups and establishment types.

Deviance—undergirded by a "turn on, tune in, drop out" mentality—was closely associated with the emergent drug culture, the sexual "revolution," supporting rights for Black citizens, and a variety of cultural innovations, including rock music. Critics did not have to search hard to find a reason to rail against performers who were so blatantly antiestablishment.

But because of the buying power of the Baby Boom generation, capitalist forces were at odds with traditional conservatism in the business world and the constant need to feed the machine. While the majority of Americans might have disapproved of hippies—the way they looked, what they believed, how they acted—the business world soon co-opted them, most noticeably by advertising campaigns, fashion, and the great American illusion-generator, Hollywood.

One of the primary forces to emerge to confront societal issues was music. Like never before the music industry rose up to feed a generation waiting to burst onto the national scene. This burgeoning power could be seen in the way advertisers courted young people, or, in a more overt demonstration, how *Time* magazine named people "Twenty-Five and Under" as "Man of the Year" in 1966. Ultimately the sheer number of young people gave them more influence than previous generations had experienced, whether it was connected to the purchasing power they wielded or the collective voice they lent to social concerns.

When the Doors formed in the fall of 1965, Jim was twenty-one, John twenty, Robby just nineteen, and Ray the elder statesman at twenty-six.

The notion that music could transform society at the individual level and as a whole permeated the Sixties. We might see this as trite today, but the idea felt alive then—palpable—and this gives context to how the Doors were formed and the philosophies they embraced. When Ray and Jim met on the beach in Santa Monica, they had been friends for a couple of years. There was a familiarity there, even though they'd been out of contact for several months. What is striking about the Doors' origin story, though, is that their common language was music.

Nowhere in Manzarek's countless retellings of the story does he make it seem that he found it strange that his young friend had been writing songs. Instead of questioning him—or ridiculing him, as a Gen Xer might imagine—Manzarek immediately asked Jim to sing them to him right there on the beach with the Pacific Ocean crashing at their feet.

Music brought people together and provided a common soundtrack in ways that were unimaginable before the Sixties. As the band would later shout: music was their only friend . . . until the end. This is why we think of the decade as an era with its own soundtrack (i.e., *Forrest Gump* is a sound as much as a film) and that it is more or less impossible to disconnect the political and social movements from the songs that gave them voice and meaning.

"All I can do is be me—whoever that is—for those people that I do play to, and not come on with them, tell them I'm something I'm not . . . the Great

Cause Fighter or the Great Lover or the Great Boy Genius. . . . Because I'm not, man. Why mislead them? That's all just Madison Avenue selling me, but it's not really selling ME, 'cause I was hip to it before I got there."
—Bob Dylan, *LA Free Press*, 1965

Jim and Ray's timing was perfect. So much had to happen to get America to the middle of the decade. The scene had been set and conditions were right for 1965 to be a launching point for the Doors and other significant cultural touchstones. Many of the mental images we have of "The Sixties" are actually based on people, incidents, and things that happened in the last three or four years of the decade. The 1960s had to percolate a range of new impulses to get to 1965, and then it roared to life in new and unexpected ways.

Still, what we remember or interpret as the "Age of Aquarius" was built on the foundation that had started the decade, a surge of great change in late 1960 and early 1961, primarily with John F. Kennedy's election to the presidency. After eight years of Dwight D. Eisenhower in the White House, JFK sparked the nation's imagination, even though the world's ills still posed threats. America also had its internal demons to contend with, from the rot of racial prejudice crippling the South to the lingering stench of McCarthyism and its sham pursuit of a Red bogeyman lurking behind every door. At the same time, the real possibility of a world-ending nuclear Armageddon pushed deep into the national psyche.

The cultural reaction against the stifling Fifties on the one side and the fear of future war with the Soviet Union on the other included folk music and youth-led attempts to jump-start a new world. The sound lilting from Greenwich Village coffeehouses and gently strummed guitars might seem far removed from the psychedelic, driving pulse of the Doors, but the fuse had to be lit. The rock through the window was thrown by Bob Dylan, a slight Minnesotan whose music would eventually transform America. This is who the members of the Doors were listening to before they launched the band, a period when their ideas about what music could do was being formed.

Dylan, born just prior to the Baby Boom, still came to exemplify the rise of that generation to a position of power. Like so many of the

Boomers, he grew into maturity with his family in a better financial position than when his parents grew up. As a result of the nation's standing in the post–World War II world, there were greater opportunities for the new generation of young people to pursue higher education, get better paying jobs, and purchase innovative consumer goods that helped make life easier. As a result, young people had a tremendous impact on music, fashion, the education system, how companies marketed and advertised products, and politics. It is not an overstatement to say that a "youth revolution" occurred in the 1960s.

Given the increase in the number of college students nationwide, it is no wonder that much of the political and social activism emerged on campuses. Given the opportunity to get an advanced education, many young people realized the inherent inequalities that existed across society, particularly for Black Americans and women. As the war in Vietnam intensified, antiwar efforts found a home on college campuses, where activists had a ready audience to counter the status quo.

The emergence of folk and rock music as anthems for these student movements sparked a synergy that empowered both the protesters and musicians. Using traditional folk techniques but updating them for the 1960s, folk musicians ushered in a new era. Suddenly, someone like Dylan, who presented himself in a simple manner—vagabond clothing, acoustic guitar, and harmonica—could gain enormous power based on his lyrics. Naturally, folk music took up its antiestablishment stance, and folk musicians stood in the vanguard of protest.

Although we view the Sixties as an utterly radical age, looking back from a slightly different perspective, the era seems just as conservative as the 1950s. For example, compare the progressive movement against the Vietnam War and racism with the popularity of nostalgic television shows like *The Beverly Hillbillies* or *Hazel*, which were filled with a mix of family values and campy humor. What is important to note for today's observer is that the popular-culture portraits of the 1960s must be balanced against the reality of the age.

There is no denying that the decade centered on the dark days of the assassination of President John F. Kennedy, race relations, Vietnam, student protests, and the murders of Martin Luther King Jr. and Robert Kennedy. On a day-to-day basis, however, many Americans found that technology, innovation, and a growing economy improved their quality of life. Perhaps the best way to assess the 1960s is in thinking about the time as a series of ebbs and flows, filled with many dramatic and often tragic events that symbolized the age, while the daily chaos of life continued to spin on.

For some people, the undercurrent left them in a strong position to fulfill their dreams and aspirations, while others experienced the decade as one of misery and madness. Folk music sprang back to life late in the decade to address some of the confusion that had people questioning the world around them.

Like its cousin, rock and roll, folk music served as one of many mass-communication channels that confronted society's challenges. Filmmakers, writers, novelists, artists, and others realized that as popular culture took a more central role in American life, they could have a more consequential voice within important socioeconomic and cultural conversations.

Six months before JFK was gunned down in Dallas, Dylan released the album *The Freewheelin' Bob Dylan*. Six weeks after the assassination, *The Times They Are A-Changin'* came out. The first turned Dylan into a megastar and central figure in the youth culture that demanded equal rights, added freedoms, and a more verdant world. Dylan's music—reflective of the folk traditions and speaking to a new generation of activists—seemed to give voice and a tune to the day's headlines. He created the soundtrack for activists and seemed like a spokesperson for a new generation.

Freewheelin' was a commercial hit, but, more important, the new album functioned as a kind of salve for a nation still lurching after the assassination of President Kennedy. Writer Robert Shelton called the album "turntable literature" and noted that "a strong sense of apocalypse dominates the album . . . Dylan, brimming with confidence, was imbuing his more complex 'stories' with larger vision and greater universality." Heady stuff for a singer who had just turned twenty-two when the record came out. Imagine Dylan's impact on young Jim Morrison, who thought himself a poet and read the Beats obsessively. Here was a singer basically his age who put poetry to music and was immediately accepted by the great writers and poets of the age.

Dylan's ability to capture the essence of the post-JFK country was shocking given that *Freewheelin'* had been recorded between August and October 1963, before the president's murder. The central theme involved those who yearn for a better life, whether it is someone facing oppression based on race or the worker attempting to keep his family afloat.

The album is fueled by the anger of the age, but even as he waited for the record to be released, Dylan began to question the status of protest songs and his role at the top of everyone's folk list. In late 1965—when the Doors were shopping their first demo from label to label in Los Angeles—a reporter asked Dylan about the generational aspect of the anthem "The Times They Are A-Changin'," and Dylan complained that it was not about age. Instead, he claimed, "those were the only words I could find to separate aliveness from deadness."

In a letter printed in *Broadside* magazine, Dylan described the toll that fame took on him personally, explaining: "I am now famous by the rules of public famiousity . . . it snuck up on me an' pulverized me . . . I never knew what was happenin'" The intensity of the media spotlight never destroyed Dylan like it did many other musicians and artists, but he increasingly recognized that such a downfall stood lurking in the wings. He may not be killed, but a different kind of threat existed, one that might take his soul.

While Dylan changed the way America would think about music's role, the Beatles' arrival took that message to the masses in a way that is almost unthinkable. One analogy might be to think about their influence like the rise of the internet or cell phones more recently. One moment, nobody had heard of these things and in seemingly the next, they were staples in people's lives.

Rock historian Greil Marcus outlined the cultural tsunami that resulted from the Beatles, explaining that their influence:

> could seem as if the Beatles had done more than change the world. It could seem as if they owned it, or as if they were it, as if every voice on earth went into theirs and was sent back to whoever it came from with more vitality, more intelligence, more heart, and more love, leaving not only the world, but individual girls and boys, men and women, changed.

Writer Candy Leonard viewed the Beatles as the unifying force of the Baby Boom generation. "Their influence," she said, "worked synergistically with other progressive cultural trends over those years, instilling in this generation a powerful belief in a happy future, filled with boundless possibility." The band from Liverpool was so instrumental in defining the Sixties that their sound became the DNA of the era, the foundation on which everything else was built.

Examining just the *Cash Box* list of number-one singles of 1965 and using that information as the foundation of an intellectual history of what influenced members of the Doors, the fingerprints of their sound and aspirations emerge in vivid colors. The Beatles had four number ones, including "Yesterday," around the time Krieger joined. In the time frame for John, the hits included "Help!" by the Beatles and "I Got You Babe" by Sonny & Cher.

As a matter of fact, the Rolling Stones' "(I Can't Get No) Satisfaction" dominated July 1965, the very month that Ray and Jim met on the beach. Certainly both were tuned into Mick and Keith's storytelling masterpiece that sounded like a short story put to words while also capturing the angst of the age. Did Ray hear the big guitar hook that opened "Satisfaction" and say to himself: "*Well, I can do that with the organ . . . let's go!*"

The magnitude of the song and its influence on the rock scene must have been on Ray's mind as he contemplated his future with Rick & the Ravens. They were playing small gigs and doing mainly cover songs, while the pop music charts were filling with original songs that emphasized storytelling and novelistic and poetic concepts. In the chilly night air on the Pacific Ocean beachfront, Manzarek couldn't have really believed that Rick & the Ravens was his future when compared to what he was hearing on the radio.

The Beatles had made huge progressive leaps in songwriting influenced by Dylan, and together they were redefining music for a legion of followers. Lyrically these were songwriters on a different level, and the lyrics-forward music that Dylan created meant that Ray had to find a solution. The intellectual leap to Morrison and his poems/lyrics is not immense. Perhaps Manzarek assessed his circumstances and grasped that he had little or nothing to lose.

The other number one of July was also influential—The Byrds' cover of "Mr. Tambourine Man," Dylan's song filled with surrealist imagery and reminiscent of French poetry. (It was the first Dylan song to reach the top of the charts.) These songs that filled the airwaves provided glimpses of possibilities to Ray and Jim.

By September, when the band was trying to find its sound and refine Jim's work into full-fledged songs, Dylan scored his own number one with "Like a Rolling Stone." The first six-minute-long song to hit the top of the charts, the powerful narrative helped fulfill his vision of the transition from folk to rock. "My words are pictures," Dylan explained, "and rock's gonna help me flesh out the colors of the pictures." The single forever changed what pop music could be, opening the door to music that extended beyond three minutes.

As inspiration for the Doors, "Like a Rolling Stone" touches many key elements they would later use, including the raw sound derived from trying to get a live feeling on tape; Dylan's use of his voice to growl, plead, manipulate, and scoff; and setting lyrical prose to music. Poet and writer Daniel Mark Epstein called the song "pure theater, theater of cruelty as Dylan had studied it in the smoke-filled bars and railroad flats of Greenwich Village." The song's power, he said, "struck a chord because most of us have experienced hatred and longed for revenge." These are words similar to the ones critics and observers used to discuss the Doors when they burst onto the scene.

Calculating Bob Dylan's musical influence would be nearly impossible, but nearly as striking would be to chart his effect on music as a business. What many people don't realize is that Dylan's first success was as a songwriter, when his manager Albert Grossman gave another one of the groups he managed—the folk trio Peter, Paul and Mary—Dylan's song "Blowin' in the Wind." By mid-July 1963, the single reached number two on the charts, sold some three hundred thousand copies in its first week, and eventually eclipsed one million. The attention the single drew catapulted Dylan to even greater heights in the folk music community, which more or less anointed him its king. The faux coronation seemed complete later that month at the Newport Folk Festival. Dylan served as everyone's main attraction.

Like Morrison would be heralded several years later, Dylan was called "a reincarnation of James Dean . . . a crushed young man whose pain seemed honest and deeply felt." Dylan, he claimed, "projected hurt and fear, in his wounded eyes and anguished voice." Other singers, watching Dylan's moves and attempting to figure out where they fit in the music world, certainly learned from their hero that charisma and likability went hand in hand with success.

Close observers might have even heard the whispers that Dylan fine-tuned his public image, from forging ties with antiwar student groups to his romantic relationship with Joan Baez, which boosted his career at a moment when her star eclipsed his. The challenge for performers and bands in the early and mid-1960s was that the music industry was evolving. Informal rules solidified that often served the machine early in a career, but then flipped the script if the musician found success. Simultaneously, other parts of the media and entertainment world got involved, essentially upping the stakes, from the teen magazines that needed content to sell copies to the countless organizations at work designing, distributing, and selling the music.

The music business was a subsection of a changing world in the Sixties that centered on mass consumption driven by advertising, marketing, and public relations. In the decades after World War II, despite growing fear of a confrontation with the Soviet Union, American consumers focused on improving their lives through a glut of new innovations, goods, and services.

For many Americans, these notions of success or the fulfillment of the American Dream meant a new car in the driveway, a well-stocked refrigerator, and a home full of the latest gizmos and gadgets. The American Dream in this age floated along on an endless sea of consumer goods piped into the nation's living rooms via television. According to advertising historian Stuart Ewen, "Mass consumption erupted, for increasing numbers, into a full-blown style of life." Television helped marketers create a space for constant advertising and selling—directly in the living rooms of eager shoppers.

Advertisers and marketers used science and psychology to determine what kinds of content would best perform the difficult task of getting consumers to reach into their wallets and purchase even more goods and services. They took their cues from popular culture, so that fads in music or film would soon be replicated in commercials. The burgeoning hippie movement and its symbols, for example, were used by multinational corporations to sell products. Record companies (many large corporations themselves) searched for artists who could sell a sound or vibe to turn a profit that helped these organizations continue making money. The wave of Beatles-like groups found or created in the wake of the band's success turned on the hope of finding "the next Beatles" who could turn a similar profit.

Can we blame Dylan for the jingly, jangly Coca-Cola songs of the late 1960s and early 1970s? Alternatively, do we criticize Paul McCartney and John Lennon for the Monkees or *The Partridge Family*? Regardless of the authenticity of Coke's calls for harmony and peace, these kinds of pleas would probably not have attempted to play on the peace movement without "The Times They Are A-Changin'" and "Blowin' in the Wind." The peace-and-love theme of these kinds of jingles captured one portion of the era yet completely overlooked the ravages of the Vietnam War. These choices were deliberate and conducted by advertising agencies that did research to identify what messages would stick with consumers best.

This conflicted era—primed by new cultural forces that hoped to turn those ideas into money—spawned the Doors. Their quick rise to fame would wedge them between the Sixties as an ideal and the consumerism that dominated the age. But, like the greats who came before them, they first had to create a sound—and they did it on the gritty Sunset Strip.

4
The Next
Whiskey
Bar

Scene: Sunset Strip, February 1966. Two friends weave their way toward the Whisky a Go Go. They see people lined up out the door and hear the sound of rock coming from within.

"The Whisky is packed, man, let's go to London Fog and check out that new band. That chick we talked to told me they were really far out. I said I'd meet her there later."

"C'mon, I hate the Fog. . . . Such a dump. There's gotta be better action down the street, like at Galaxy. Let's check that out."

"Just a couple minutes, I want to find her, then we'll split."

Weaving through a crowd gathered halfway up the block, the two friends talked to two dudes selling acid and another nervously pushing weed. The cops were out earlier, but didn't seem bothered, as long as you were smoking filtered cigarettes with the logo visible. A group of short-hairs wandered aimlessly, saucer-eyed as they peeked toward the clubs, a beefy bouncer standing guard at nearly every awning that marks the location of one joint from another door.

Looking up, they see a red banner that is visible for at least a block on the Strip: The Doors from Venice Beach. *The Doors? What kind of name is that?* the naysayer thinks.

Three immediate sensory experiences hit you as you enter London Fog: it is dark, hot, and smells like beer and cigarettes crushed into a carpet and left for several months. Looking around, you see that there aren't many people, maybe a couple dozen, but it feels tight. Swirls and groovy designs line the ceiling and pick up what little light shines in, but the English theme really doesn't work, despite the newspaper wallpaper, fake brick on the wall, and images of faux royalty scattered about. Just like at the Whisky, a young woman dances in a cage. You wonder if that is what all the British clubs are like.

Now the reason you're there—the girl. *"She's in here somewhere. . . ."*

Suddenly, you hear the deep thud of an organ note, then more. Focusing on the stage, you see the band fiddling with their instruments. The guy behind the keyboards looks like a professor. The drummer blasts a quick beat on the snare, then stops. He has a blank look on his face, but his muttonchop sideburns make him seem regal. The guitarist picks at the amp next to him, then slides his fingers up the neck. Out front is a skinny guy who clamps both hands on the microphone. Eyes closed, he looks like a lot of the actors around town.

"Well, this must be the Doors."

The band is framed by an ugly, cheap-looking curtain behind them. It looks like a strong breeze off the Pacific could topple the group and knock down the entire stage. An amp rests at the singer's feet. A little chain, only about shin-high for the band, but about shoulder-high for patrons, demarcates the front of the stage. The padded stage perimeter must be in case people dancing get too close to the stage. Not a chance of that happening tonight—crowd's too small.

"I want you to rock me," the singer suddenly blurts out, eyes still closed. The organ and drum drop in behind, while the guitarist knocks out a few chords.

"Bluesy," you say to your friend. He smiles for a moment and hands you a beer. The singer pulls out a harmonica and blares away. *Not bad!* Then you recognize the song, it's "Rock Me." B.B. King's version got a lot of play a couple years ago. *Not bad at all for a bunch of white guys!* The beer is cold and the moment is almost perfect.

You never did find that girl. . . .

After being turned down by every nightclub in town (sometimes auditioning multiple times), the Doors were hired at London Fog, a bar attempting to capitalize on the British Invasion kicked off by the Beatles and sustained by American record execs who wanted to make money on the mania. The gimmick wasn't fooling anyone, but the Sunset Strip surged with teens and young people, music fans, and other curious onlookers in search of fun. Most observers remembered the club as a refuge for low-lifes, drunks, gangsters, and people who couldn't or wouldn't frequent more-reputable establishments.

Thinking back on their time at the Fog, Densmore said, "The stage was so fucking high, you needed an oxygen mask. I was worried about Jim falling." And who could forget the dancing girl, he laughed: "Across the way was a cage with Rhonda Layne, the go-go girl. She was slightly overweight and wore a miniskirt and go-go boots, doing the twist or the frug." Layne must have been hearing that danceable beat in her head, because the fledgling band had a catalog of about forty songs back then, most of them blues covers that would have made dancing difficult.

We don't know how much she was paid to endure the onslaught, but the band members made five dollars each on weeknights and ten on the weekends, playing multiple sets from nine in the evening until around two a.m., six nights a week. Unlike the others, Jim had no one to lend him financial support, so what seems like meager pay by today's measures certainly must have been riches to him. Five dollars in 1966 equates to about fifty today, so they were not going to get rich at London Fog, but it was a start. For the first time since graduating from college, Morrison had a bit of spending money.

More significantly, the gig enabled the Doors to practice in front of a live audience, even if some nights there weren't many people there. Show after show, the band slipped onto a familiar path for successful musicians—developing a style and their own original songs through repetition and experiment. Explaining how the Doors created music back then, Ray said, "The lyrics always come first, then we get together and everyone makes his contribution." Next came "chord changes and melody ideas" he and Robby would add, thus fleshing out the body of the composition. Densmore's "rhythm ideas" then created a heartbeat. "In effect, each song sort of evolves," Manzarek said.

Another evolution took place as Jim came into his own, first overcoming his natural shyness. In the early gigs he couldn't even muster up the confidence to look at the audience, so he did what little singing he could croak out with his back to them. "He needed time to find his voice, both literally and figuratively," Robby said. "The Fog is where Jim abandoned the lightweight head voice he used on the original demo and built up the full-chested howl he became known for."

What we might call "liquid courage" today was another tool Morrison used to battle his inhibitions—but he went one step further, combining an increasing amount of booze with large quantities of acid. Allegedly, the young singer was smoking pot during the day and then doing acid at the shows. Along the rumor mill of Sunset Strip, news of Jim's manic energy and odd stage manner caused a stir among music fans. It wasn't overnight, but the Doors started to carve out a following. Manzarek, though, assessed the gig differently: "Nobody came in for the three months we were there."

Between sets, they snuck down the street a few blocks to the Whisky a Go Go, imagining a future where they might play there, the mecca of clubs on Sunset Strip. That prospect took a hit in late April, however, when Columbia dropped the band. Billy James simply couldn't find a producer to put out the requisite singles to kick the long-term part of the deal into effect.

Playing about thirty hours a week enabled the Doors to craft a sound that was wholly unique and gave Morrison time to grow into his voice, which some would later say was the best yell in rock history. Sometimes hard work earns lucky breaks, and that seemed to be the band's fate.

Depending on which story you believe, the Doors were either fired by the Fog's owners because they didn't draw patrons and the bar was running out of money or a fight broke out (some say Jim being the instigator), which was blamed on Morrison, and led to them getting canned. Either way, the Doors were out of a job. Manzarek's panic could have come from any one of them: "My god, what are we gonna do now?"

There are several versions of what happened next. Some accounts are that Ronnie Haran, the Whisky talent booker, happened into the Fog to hear the Doors for herself given all the buzz about Morrison (on the night of their very last performance there nonetheless). Another version is that the band members, particularly Jim, kept asking her—begging, really—to give them a shot. Manzarek chalked it up to the former, explaining that Haran "immediately fell in love with Jim, loved the music." Either version, though, ends with the same good news—the Doors were the new house band at the Whisky, the most vaunted and hottest club on Sunset Strip.

Without Ronnie's intervention, the Doors might have faded. There are reports that she and Jim shacked up for a while, while others claim Morrison was just crashing on her couch. In any event, Ronnie got him prepped for the Whisky: "I knew Jim had star quality the minute I saw him [but] he didn't have a pot to piss in. I had to dress him, get him some T-shirts and turtlenecks at the Army-Navy store." Hiring the Doors was a huge risk, particularly given the number of famous bands playing the club. Lots of egos, money, and livelihoods were on the line.

Playing to a handful of fans and barflies every night at the Fog was a necessary step in the band's evolution, but it didn't fulfill their collective aspirations. Yes, they were making music, but they needed listeners. When they wandered down the block and stood outside the door at the Whisky a Go Go, they found their mecca.

The Whisky was the coolest spot for live music in Hollywood. Peeking inside, Jim, John, Robby, and Ray got a glimpse of women dancing in a cage hoisted above the dance floor, decked out in matching midriff-baring, ruffled getups. The packed house was usually filled with a broad swath of hipsters and lots of clean-cut college kids and young people (many in sport coats and ties). But it was the music that set the Whisky apart from LA's other clubs. The hottest bands in the world played the Whisky. It was a mandatory date when bands hit the West Coast.

By late May, about seven months after Robby joined the band, they started their run as house band at the Whisky. The larger crowds helped the band improve quickly. "We played almost every night for three or four months," Krieger said. "We'd play our songs every night and see how the audience reacted. When you play it live, you get a sense of what works and what doesn't." The musicians had instant feedback that they could then compare to earlier reactions, while Jim could work through and refine his stage persona. Morrison agreed: "We were creating our music, ourselves, every night, starting with a few outlines, maybe a few words for a song that gradually accrued particles of meaning and movement."

Jim called that much-needed energy between the band and the crowd "beautiful tension," which came from the need to perform well for patrons, but to do so with a sense of freedom and spontaneity. "I can put in a full day's work [rehearsing], go home and take a shower, change clothes, then play two or three sets at the Whisky, man, and I love it. The way an athlete loves to run, to keep in shape."

While the residency at the Whisky exposed the band to large crowds and gave them a chance to hone their onstage performance by watching headliners do their thing, they continued to refine their work at numerous other gigs. They would play just about anywhere they could, hungry for success and exposure.

The notion that they had to get as many repetitions in as they could humanly perform gives a new perspective to the business side of the band.

Morrison might have upped his alcohol intake and drug consumption, but when it came to perfecting their style, Jim took the craft-making seriously—or, well, considering Morrison's state of mind, as earnestly as he could.

For example, just days after they first auditioned at the Whisky, the Doors played the Warner Playhouse in LA, doing sets between two and four in the morning. An advertisement for the shows called them "total entertainment" but also revealed that they shared the stage with "Claudette," featuring "exotic dancing and attitudes." They also supported Ray by performing at a student film exhibition in Royce Hall Auditorium at UCLA.

Music insiders began whispering about the Doors as a potential breakout band, despite the Columbia debacle of scoring a record deal but then never actually cutting a single. Arthur Lee of the eclectic band Love was an early supporter. He asked the Doors to open for the group on May 12 and 13 at their gigs at a short-lived club called Brave New World. Although he would later resent the Doors for eclipsing his band, Lee was at the center of the group's next big evolution—getting a new deal with Elektra Records, founded by music insider Jac Holzman.

Like a scene out of a movie, Ronnie Haran glided her gorgeous white convertible into a spot near the gate at the airport. Well into the evening, she was there to pick up Holzman, who was arriving from New York. Love was playing the Whisky that night and the label president wanted to check in on the band, one of top ones in his stable. "I was beat, but I went," Holzman explained. "Arthur urged me to stick around for the next band. Whoever they were, Arthur had a high opinion of them, and I had a very high opinion of Arthur's opinion, so I stayed." That band was the Doors.

The record exec was grumpy and tired. It had been a long trip and he was still on East Coast time. When the Doors came on, they didn't know how important this performance might be. And whether it was an off night for the band or just Jac's jet lag, he wasn't impressed. "Jim was lovely to look at, but there was no command," he remembered. "Perhaps I was thinking too conventionally, but their music had none of the rococo ornamentation with which a lot of rock and roll was being embellished—remember, this was still the era of the Beatles and *Revolver*, circa 1966."

Unexpectedly, however, Holzman found himself thinking about the Doors, even after he had initially written them off. He ended up seeing them four straight evenings and on the fourth night, the band showed him a new future. "Jim generated an enormous tension with his performance, like a black hole, sucking the energy of the room into himself." He decided, "This was no ordinary rock-and-roll band. . . . When I heard, really heard, Manzarek's baroque organ line under 'Light My Fire,' I was ready to sign them."

If there was a challenge with signing a record deal it was that the Doors had no lawyers or business acumen. While they searched for the right attorney, however, they stayed at the Whisky and continued to work on their songs. They learned from the headliners they opened for, but the real goal, Densmore said, "was to blow the headliners off the stage." Some nights they did, but others Jim showed up late or too drunk, ultimately upsetting club owner Elmer Valentine, who threatened to fire them almost nightly. With a sheepish, aw-shucks smirk while putting on his best Southern drawl, Morrison would apologize. He gradually won over the older man, despite never actually relenting when it came to his bad behavior.

The entire summer and fall 1966, the Doors learned at the feet of big-time bands, like Them, featuring Van Morrison. Although soft-spoken away from the microphone, Van was often drunk and angry onstage. Jim aped several of his moves, including slamming the mic stand into the floor. Of Van, Robby recalled: "In the early Whisky days he was a terror. I mean you'd be afraid to come anywhere near the stage—drunk as hell, throwing the mic around. . . . He had some real devils inside." Both Morrisons swore up a storm. A highlight of the run was when they sang together on "In the Midnight Hour" and "Gloria," which had long been one of Jim's favorite tunes.

While they picked up tips and tricks from bands that headlined, the Doors continued to evolve musically. They created an ethos based on Jim Morrison's long-held beliefs in the power of violence. Their sound thumped and thundered, reflecting their era and projecting it out to audiences that were unnerved by its energy. Jim knew what people wanted. "America was conceived in violence. Americans are attracted to violence," he later explained. "They attach themselves to processed violence, out of cans. They're TV-hypnotized . . . they're emotionally dead." The attraction–revulsion theme centering on elemental forces of light, dark, love, hate, life, and death would have been impossible for most bands to implement, but the Doors were staking their future on that principle.

Although the Doors broke new ground with their sound, some musicians didn't get Jim or what the band was trying to do. In early August, the Rolling Stones dropped by the Whisky to hear the Doors. Reports are that the British megastars were not impressed. This initial meeting set in motion a complicated relationship between the two bands. What many observers noticed during the Whisky stint was that the Doors could be really, really good or putrid, sometimes on the same night. Frequently this assessment depended on how much booze Jim drank or how many drugs he downed.

For example, the first time Holzman took Paul Rothchild, his best producer, to see the band, Rothchild was flabbergasted. In front of a relatively sparse crowd, he remembered:

> The Doors opened and I heard one of the worst sets of music I have ever heard in my life. Knowing that the record company always gets to hear the bad sets, and that I had just traveled across the country to hear them, I stayed and heard one of the greatest sets of music I have ever heard in my life!

A couple weeks after the Rolling Stones heard them, Robby, John, and Ray showed up for their early gig, but Jim never did. After the requisite hand-wringing and arguments with Valentine and co-owner Phil Tanzini, they went on with Ray doing all the singing. Then, the owners dropped an ultimatum, find Morrison for the second set or they would fire the entire band on the spot.

Ray and John found Jim at the Alta Cienega Hotel. They banged on his door until he peeked out. As he had done so many times before, the singer had taken so much acid that he could barely stand. The drummer and organist got him dressed as quickly as possible, trying to talk him down from his trip. They believed that if Jim was onstage, they would be able to save their jobs.

The three Doors got to the Whisky just in time to prop Jim up, although he was mainly incoherent. In their last set, however, Morrison recovered a bit. Allegedly he had taken ten or twenty times what constituted a single hit of LSD, so much in fact that one wonders if he had deliberately tried to overdose. They kicked into the haunting "The End," a crowd favorite and perhaps the truest representation of just how different the Doors were than every other band on the planet.

The next ten to fifteen minutes are etched in rock history. Morrison locked into the spoken word section of the song and recited the Oedipal mantra about killing his father and having sex with his mother. Regardless of the origin of this improvisation or its effect on the quiet, stunned crowd, Tanzini and Valentine had ultimate authority in the Whisky. Tanzini stormed into the green room and fired the Doors immediately. Given Tanzini's alleged mob connections, Morrison should—yet again—have been thankful that he made it out with his head still attached to his body. Yet in a strange twist, several sources, including Krieger and Morrison, indicate that the Doors did play the Whisky for at least another day or so.

Without mentioning that he was tripping at the time, Jim later spoke at length about the "Oedipus thing." The song evolved from a "goodbye song" written about Mary Werbelow, his first true love, to something he called "a little more serious." That night at the Whisky, he reported, "Something clicked. I realized what the whole song was about, what it had been leading up to. It was powerful. It just happened. They fired us the next day."

Getting canned unleashed Morrison's inner demons, and a dark prince emerged from the ashes of that scorching performance. There are any number of ways to read this incident, though, that paint Jim poorly. First, he let his band down multiple times in the same day by doing the drugs, skipping out on the gig, and—most egregiously—taking the song in a direction that he had to have known would get them fired. In other words, he put himself ahead of the band's welfare.

Some people, like Ronnie Haran, seemed to expect this behavior from Jim, perhaps thinking it was part of his developing persona. "He was getting crazy, taking acid every day. He was obsessed with death, never did anything in moderation, a consumptive personality," she explained. "When we parted, he said, 'I'm gonna be dead in two years.'"

Interestingly, Morrison's bandmates didn't seem to hold these antics against him. Looking back on the importance of the Whisky era, they viewed it as critical in their singer coming into his own. Judgment about excessive drug and alcohol use didn't appear to be part of their ethos at that point in the band's history. Actually, Robby framed the discussion within the popularity of the song, indicating that the Oedipal version that night "was the loudest burst of applause we'd ever gotten."

On November 15, 1966, the Doors finally signed with Elektra, committing to seven albums, and Holzman promised the label would market and promote them heavily. The signing ended speculation that the band was being pursued by every label in LA. Jim recalled, "People said everyone in town was trying to sign us up, but it really wasn't true . . . in fact, Jac Holzman's might have been the only concrete offer we had . . . there's no question we weren't that much in demand."

In a little more than a year, the Doors had a record deal. Pamela Des Barres, who would later become a celebrated muse and kind of professional groupie, spoke for a legion of fans that discovered the Doors in 1966:

> The word was out on the street that everyone had to see this lead singer because there had never been anything like him. . . . He looked like a Greek god gone wrong, with masses of dark brown curls and a face that sweaty dreams are made of. . . . There was no modern sexy American icon at that time and he instantly became that for me and all the girls I knew and we never missed them. I saw the Doors play a hundred times."

What happened for the band was just as revelatory. What the Doors created in that burst of inspiration—as well as when feeding off the energy of live audiences—was a singular sound, even in an era driven by Dylan, the Beatles, the Rolling Stones, and the many groups emerging from San Francisco.

John Densmore summed up the outcome, explaining how the pieces came together: "The musical background each of us brought to our partnership fed us well and fertilized our unique feel and sound." For Robby Krieger: "Mainly we learned to be ourselves." From his perspective, 1966 was essential: "Thanks to that spring at the Fog and that summer at the Whisky, we improved individually and as a group, but Jim's transformation was the most noticeable, and the most crucial."

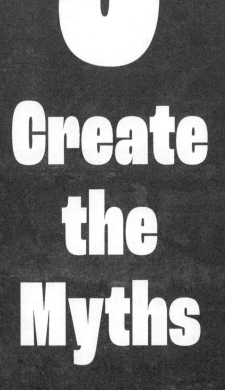

5

Create the Myths

When the Doors entered the studio to record their debut album it was essentially Ray's band. He had created it with Jim. Then John joined, and then Robby. The keyboardist was also the senior member in terms of age, but that was distinctly not a hip rationale for calling the shots in late 1966. Instead, the bandmates agreed on a Three Musketeers type of decision-making process—decisions were made as a foursome, unanimously or not at all.

Still, someone had to nudge the band, set the tone, and that naturally fell to Ray. Of all the various groups he, John, and Robby had been in before the Doors, Manzarek had the most success. He had the practice space. It all lined up. Most important, it was Ray's vision of what the Doors could be that drove them all toward a collective future. It was as if he willed the Lizard King into existence, as well as the tight trio that would back him. This was the path to rock stardom—he could feel it.

Decades later, even though we know much of the history, it's amazing how Ray saw the way his young band would capture the zeitgeist. He later explained:

We knew once the people heard us we'd be unstoppable. We were making our music for the people. To turn each other on. Both us and them. The transcendental elevation of the psyche through the manipulation of sound waves. We knew what the people wanted: the same thing the Doors wanted. Freedom.

What gave Ray an edge was his age and film-school education. As a filmmaker—one who other UCLA students looked up to—he knew how to map a sequence of events to create a product. Jim's lyrics provided the script; Ray attached them to a sound. The bonus was that Manzarek found his leading man.

Manzarek's vision, according to Evan Palazzo, piano player and bandleader of the critically acclaimed jazz band the Hot Sardines, was "almost like the way Bach would write with variations on a theme that would take you places, as opposed to going around and around on a chorus." Evolving from that style helped the Doors depart on flights of fancy on solos and create the jam-band sound. "It sounds so simple, until you try to play it," Palazzo explains. "If you're ever foolish enough to do that, you realize that like all great music, it's incredibly intricate."

Over the long nights at London Fog, the Whisky, and playing late-night gigs around Los Angeles, the Doors created the foundation—a sound no one could replicate that was instantly recognizable. Robby, always a bit modest, claimed that he "stumbled ass-backward into a unique style. It wasn't a conscious effort to sound different. I was just too lazy to properly learn how to sound the same."

Ray, always the voice of the times, said: "The communal mind would run the magic. . . . We roared and we rocked." Holzman's decision to team the band with producer Paul Rothchild and engineer Bruce Botnick created the environment that brought the magic to life. They built the sound on Ray's organ work—his unique talent to play the bass with his left hand and solo with his right. Like a great jazz trio, John and Robby matched their styles to his yet still maintained their own individual sounds. "It's clusterings," Palazzo said of Manzarek's solo style. "It's hard to pick up all the notes, because it's deep, complex, and very hard to play." As a result, "you never hear people imitating Manzarek because he's impossible to imitate. You can play a couple notes, but that's it."

The final component was Morrison's singing. Even Ray couldn't have envisioned that transformation in just a year. Vocalists don't typically decide in an acid-filled summer that they are going to become a rock star and front a world-class band, no matter how inspiring Elvis or Dylan were.

Densmore called Jim's growth "special." He recalled:

> At first, nerves made his voice thin, but eventually, after about a year of rehearsals, it developed into a deep baritone. Then there was his scream. It sounded like someone being crucified, a moan from the bowels of his soul. For a guy who had never sung before he met his bandmates, his voice was a huge gift from the other world.

From the performance Rothchild had seen at the Whisky—one he called among the greatest he had ever witnessed—he knew he needed to reproduce the live sound on record. He and Botnick had to not only construct the right environment technically to capture the material but also get a new band with four young men into the proper groove to lay it down.

The Doors looked up to Rothchild but, even though they hit it off personally, he was still essentially their boss. Nerves were an issue, balancing anxiety with excitement. The tight-knit band had to let in two new members, which they did, trusting that Rothchild and Botnick would help them to make the best album possible.

Every record deal is a gamble. The band knew the stakes, but, according to Manzarek, they were "dying to make it." What he knew was a "dream come true" necessitated that all the pieces come together, from the recording sessions to publicity and marketing efforts.

If there was a challenge it was Jim's tendency toward excess. His bandmates had learned to cope with this aspect of their singer's lifestyle, but when every minute counts, resentment can form. Ray explained that Jim "knew he would be forgiven any excess." Did Jim use that to his advantage to validate his wild-child extravagances? That's a hard question to answer. "He was just too charming and too damned much fun to be with for us to ever hold a grudge against him for more than a couple of hours. And he knew it," Manzarek claimed. "He'd give you that sly grin of his, and you were hooked. . . . A fool for his charm." But, as he knew, pardoning one extreme incident meant that Jim would up the ante the next time.

What Ray remembered more than Jim's indiscretions, though, was his happiness in the studio—a happiness they all felt in the face of their good fortune. Overtaken with bliss, Morrison frequently danced out of the vocals booth, doing the shaman shake (that he would later make famous) and slamming on a maraca.

"We didn't start out with such big ideas. We thought we were going to be just another pop group, but then something happened when we recorded 'The End.' We saw that what we were doing was more important than just a hit song. We were writing serious music and performing it in a very dramatic way. 'The End' is like going to see a movie when you already know the plot. It's a timeless piece of material. . . . It was then that we realized we were different from other groups. We were playing music that would last for years, not weeks."

—Jim Morrison

Jim's lyrics, melded with the tight trio behind him, led to songs that could be at once chilling, joyful, mysterious, and dreamlike. There wasn't really a model for being *both* a pop hit-maker and a hard-rock band with jazz, blues, and classical influences. Perhaps the closest was the Rolling Stones. Next was the Doors.

The first single would be "Break On Through"—a song that would launch the album, but, more important, become the band's credo. The lyrics centered on Jim's desire to push boundaries, get messy emotionally and physically, and leap—sometimes without looking—into the dark night, consequences be damned. The single also set the tone for how the band would sound musically: big organ sound driving the beat with drums and guitar diving in and out, and all entwined with Morrison's vocals, whether a soft purr or aggressive yell.

Krieger preferred an understated style, which contrasted to other guitarists, like Jimi Hendrix and Jimmy Page, who would later usher in the "guitar god" era.

Of course, we know what happened when "Light My Fire" hit. The Doors proved a hard-rock band could also write unforgettable pop songs. Most of the early tunes were from Jim's notebooks full of lyrics and poetry. But when he asked the others to pitch in, Robby wrote "Light My Fire." He tried to make it different from their other songs and it worked. Krieger later explained, "Most of our tunes were three-chord songs. . . . So I decided that I was going to write a song with a lot of chords. Nobody was doing that in rock and roll at the time. I wanted to be different."

Beyond the first singles and "The End," the debut also featured pulsating blues-rock in "Soul Kitchen"; the crooning, ephemeral "The Crystal Ship"; the decadent "Alabama Song (Whisky Bar)," an ode to 1920s, avant-garde Berlin; and the depraved anthem "Back Door Man."

This lineup is the rock music equivalent of the 1927 New York Yankees or 1996 Chicago Bulls. Song after song, their style had been gutted out over two years of gigs and rehearsals. Later, Jim explained that "the whole arrangement and actual generation of the piece would happen night after night, day after day, either in rehearsal or in clubs."

After the exuberance of recording the album, the Doors hit the road again, making their first trip to New York City around Halloween. For a band out of LA with no national pull, the NYC shows had considerable ramifications. Being in New York also gave the Doors the opportunity to work with Rothchild as he mixed the record.

They had been booked at the Ondine, a tiny club in Manhattan on Fifty-Ninth Street where celebrities and the city's elite went to let loose. The hippest person on the scene was Andy Warhol, accompanied by his many acolytes and hangers-on—the beautiful people—but others included Jackie Kennedy, Jackie Gleason, and a horde of models, actors, and glam devotees. The Ondine basically operated as a private discotheque long before disco would become all the rage, a kind of fashionable speakeasy with go-go dancers, frenzied dance music, and a strange cast of characters. The basement locale was an odd place for ritzy socialites to frequent, tucked under a bridge in an ominous part of the city just three blocks from the East River.

Brad Pierce, the club manager, had connections in the music business, so he began booking live acts. Warhol later claimed that the Doors were booked there because a female deejay who had moved from LA knew the band and urged Pierce to bring them east. To New York audiences, the Doors were billed as the hottest underground band going. Enough people were bicoastal and had heard whispers about the group. Everyone wanted to see the lead singer.

The Doors played gigs at the Ondine over the course of the next month. Similar to London Fog, the club, named after the famous racing yacht Ondine, had a cramped stage that contrasted with its nautical theme.

Jim met Warhol, of course, but the iconic artist was reportedly so nervous about the encounter that he spent an evening mumbling to himself and awkwardly avoiding the singer. Eventually Warhol overcame his stage fright, probably at the sight of so many women mobbing Morrison while he stood at the bar between sets. "It was love at first sight on Andy's part," Ray said later.

Introducing himself to one young beauty when the band first arrived at the club on Halloween, Morrison told her his name was "James Phoenix," a name that Ray claimed he always wanted to use because it sounded mysterious. Jim fell in love with New York immediately. Manzarek explained: "Here, finally, was the opportunity for a serious debauch." The entire band looked on in wonder at the great American mecca. Ray recalled, "Strange days had found us!"

Jim met Pamela Courson in early 1966, when the band returned from New York. The two moved in together around the time he celebrated his twenty-third birthday. They lived in a little apartment in Laurel Canyon, a sleepy area that attracted a lot of musicians, hippies, and others trying to escape the hectic day-to-day life in Los Angeles. (Jim later immortalized the time in the song "Love Street.")

By all accounts, the young couple seemed to be the male–female versions of one another. According to mutual friend and sometime-housemate Mirandi Babitz, they sometimes went too far, which she described as "very dangerous things too," including "putting the car on the railroad tracks or driving with their eyes closed down Mulholland at night while on acid." Pretty much everyone who knew Jim and Pam agreed that they shared an intense interest in drugs, rabble-rousing, and pushing each other to the limit emotionally and physically.

Though the band had an album in the can, Morrison didn't have much money, so he and Pam spent time freewheeling through the area, just attempting to break on through. They had live-in houseguests—pretty common in the era—and any money they cobbled together went into the communal pot for drugs, food, and whatever necessities they needed. Around that same time, John and Robby finally moved out of their parents' places and got ones of their own. Jim would visit them, especially when he just needed someone to talk to or a place to hide out and let his mind wander.

What we now think of as the Sixties was really coming into form in 1966, but it would blossom fully the following year. Even Manzarek couldn't have imagined what the Summer of Love held in store for the Doors. That year would fulfill every wish that Jac Holzman and Paul Rothchild had for the band when they signed them.

6
Summer
of
Love

As 1967 began, "Jim Morrison" was a guy on your bowling team if you lived in Charleston, West Virginia, or one of the many local realtors hustling for business in Sandusky, Ohio. In other words, the name itself had yet to enter the national consciousness. The world had yet to meet the future Lizard King.

After their first album was released on January 4, 1967, the Doors remained little more than a really popular local Los Angeles band. In contrast to today's blockbuster mentality in which all the marketing and publicity efforts focus on the release date and immediate success, the self-titled record progressed steadily on the charts. For four young men hungry for success, a new album meant playing wherever they could play and being seen wherever they could be seen.

Whether looking at album sales, considering concert tickets sold, or listening to the radio, it would be impossible to separate the youth-oriented marketplace from its musical soundtrack. The Baby Boom generation had more disposable income than any generation in American history, and they used it to put music at the center of their lives. The celebrity industry responded in kind, unleashing an army of publicists, advertisers, and marketers hoping to turn a new band into the next Beatles.

The Elektra promotional team had a challenge with the Doors. The band didn't look or sound like anything else in the market, which is always a problem because potential audiences can't place the hot new thing. Awareness was key—they had to get people to sample the Doors.

Promotion had begun before the album's release when the band made their first live TV appearance on a show called *Shebang* that ran on the hometown station KTLA on Sunday nights. Hosted by Casey Kasem and produced by Dick Clark, the show featured teenagers dancing to popular acts, similar to *American Bandstand*, which had launched in the Fifties. Local versions like *Shebang* were becoming more popular as more teens meant more bands. Although a live appearance, the Doors lip-synched "Break On Through," the initial single.

The band was already known locally for their psychedelic sound and Jim's stage antics, but the Doors looked tame on the dance show. The stage setup was a colorful mix of Day-Glo yellows, reds, and oranges, mixed in with a bunch of houseplants. According to the other band members, Morrison barely attempted to lip-synch, but it wasn't out of arrogance. "We were clearly nervous," John said. "I mean, Jim won't even look at the camera or anything." The singer was a long way from becoming the Lizard King.

A year later the Doors would be the hottest band in America.

With the first album in stores, the Doors toured to support the release. California was the focus, naturally, but they immediately went to San Francisco, which was dicey for any LA band. At different ends of the state, the two cities shared little in terms of style and culture and many music insiders believed a band couldn't be popular in both places.

The initial shows were good, but the Doors opened for more popular bands like the Young Rascals and the Grateful Dead. In their off-hours, the band soaked up San Francisco's culture. At one point Jim traveled up to the state capitol in Sacramento and sat through three showings of *Casablanca*, missing a Friday night show.

Part of the band's education in the City by the Bay took place at The Human Be-In, a festival featuring music, activists, and spirituality in Golden Gate Park. Twenty thousand people had gathered to protest a California law banning LSD that had passed the previous fall. The Doors played elsewhere throughout the weekend but weren't established enough to play the festival.

Alongside famous poets like Allen Ginsberg and Michael McClure, activist and educator Timothy Leary called for the crowd to "Turn on, tune in, drop out," a phrase that would become legendary and epito-mize the psychedelic era. Leary's mantra and the large crowds that filled the Haight-Ashbury neighborhood caught the national media's atten-tion, which brought the hippie movement into the homes of millions of Americans via news reports and TV segments.

It's impossible to gauge the impact the Doors had on listeners in San Francisco, but their sound was certainly alien to the trippy vibe that local fans loved. On the surface, Ray, Robby, Jim, and John seemed to fit in as openers for the Dead, but Jerry Garcia disliked Morrison almost immedi-ately. According to writer Dennis McNally, "Morrison struck him as the embodiment of Los Angeles . . . the triumph of style without substance. The Doors had no bassist and consequently sounded thin to him, and Morrison's imitation of Mick Jagger did not impress him."

A couple of months later and after many more shows, the Doors returned to San Francisco as headliners, playing prestigious venues like the Avalon Ballroom. Morrison's transformation had begun. His dark persona surfaced in all-black clothing, and he let his hair grow longer and wilder. Some observers noted that local fans adopted Jim's style, showing up to concerts mimicking his appearance, despite the lighter, more colorful clothing that was popular in the city. As a band, the Doors won over Northern California crowds with their raw intensity and emotion.

However, as a new group, the Doors did face challenges, particularly when "Break On Through" stalled on the singles charts. Elektra President Jac Holzman had put significant resources behind the song, including cutting a video to be shown on local television stations and erecting the famous Sunset Strip billboard introducing the album to LA.

Holzman would later defend his decision to release "Break On Through" as a way to get people excited about the Doors, but without placing too much emphasis on sales figures or chart position. "Get the marketplace prepared," he explained, which included sending the video out to small markets that had dance shows but were too tiny for the band to visit. "We sent out a lot of them," Holzman recalled.

While the first single didn't catch the public's imagination in a way to make it a hit, Doors fans called FM radio stations requesting "Light My Fire," despite the song being over seven minutes long. Holzman, producer Paul Rothchild, and the band members knew they had to create a radio-friendly version of the song if they wanted to capitalize on the newfound interest.

In late April, Rothchild got the song to three minutes by removing several solo jams in the middle of the longer version. Elektra released "Light My Fire" and "The Crystal Ship." The stripped-down single would soon change the band's trajectory—and rock history. John Densmore later explained how the intro captured listeners' souls: "It's a circle of fifths, played in a baroque [Bach-like] style. This keyboard part is permanently stamped on everyone's brain. We will never forget it."

John, Ray, and Robby had watched Jim's struggles with drugs and alcohol from the beginning of their time together. None of them were innocent when it came to drugs or booze, and the self-help–addiction treatment culture we have today didn't exist. Looking back at the shows in the spring, one wishes that the tight-knit trio would have read Jim's behavior a little better or that the culture then understood addiction and its consequences.

Co-headlining with Jefferson Airplane, the Doors played for the largest crowd of their career at the Cheetah on the Santa Monica Pier—more than three thousand fans. Jim punctuated the appearance by falling off the eight-foot-high stage during the show. In their first headlining gigs at Bill Graham's Fillmore Auditorium in June, Morrison was late and drunk, which caused friction and led to several shouting matches with the legendary promoter. In retaliation—an older authority figure had scolded him—Jim flailed the microphone around over his head like a lasso. He swung it out over the crowed. When Graham intervened, Morrison let the microphone go, a David-and-Goliath move that resulted in the older man being whacked in the head.

John, Ray, and Robby were in a tough position. They knew they couldn't control their singer. He would have rebelled even more and viewed such an intervention as shattering their bond as a band. The proverbial writing on the wall had to be there, yet they seemed powerless to alter the inevitable. Surely the good shows gave them hope, and if their wild singer needed to act like a rock god, they could indulge him.

An early supporter, Eileen Kaufman, critic at the *Los Angeles Free Press*, lauded the band's development, calling them "a phenomenon." Jim, she contended, would "flip the kids and psych out all his listeners. . . . He has the appearance: aesthetic, hungry, sad, soulful." After watching him at several headlining performances, Kaufman determined, "he is a poet to be reckoned with." She gave equal praise to the other band members—John for being like the great jazz drummers, Ray for creating the foundation that helped the band sizzle, and Robby for merging his guitar perfectly with Jim's voice.

Across Northern California promoters came up with a new concept— the music festival. On a beautiful day in early June in Marin County, across the Golden Gate Bridge from San Francisco, a sizable crowd was ready to enjoy the day at the nation's first music festival. The stage was framed by seven large flags, each about twenty feet tall and four feet wide. They featured various peace symbols, the yin and yang, and smiling moons. Behind the flags was Mount Tamalpais, an unmistakable attraction in the heart of Marin that rises to twenty-five hundred feet and features lush trees. The crowd jammed the amphitheater, a sea of bodies that rose up hillside—a mix of hippies from the Haight and college students from the many Bay Area universities. Those down front danced along—when they could find space wide enough to let them shimmy and sway to the music.

In contrast to their dark image, the band members were dressed in summer colors. Jim wore tight tan pants, a leather belt, and a striped, button-down shirt. Robby's bright red guitar stands out in photos of the event, as does Ray being set up on Jim's left, opposite their typical configuration. At times clutching the mic stand tightly, but also snapping along to the beat and dancing wildly, Morrison seemed to be enjoying the day, weather, and crowd in the kind of rock festival that would come to define his generation. Promoters sold thirty thousand tickets with all proceeds going to the Hunters Point Child Care Service. A giant forty-foot-high Buddha balloon greeted festivalgoers near the amphitheater.

From San Francisco, the band flew to New York City. They had a series of shows, including a three-week stint at Steve Paul's Scene, one of the hippest clubs in the city, on West 46th Street. On any given night, you could see Andy Warhol and his acolytes, as well as photographer Linda Eastman (who later married Paul McCartney) and singer Tiny Tim, who opened for the headlining bands. According to some sources, Morrison had a dalliance with Eastman during the residency.

Although the Scene was the place for celebrities and others to be seen, the club was small and dark. The band performed on a tiny, slightly elevated stage that barely had enough room for them and their equipment. Behind Krieger was a dingy fireplace and a graffiti-laden backdrop that made the stage look more like a dorm room than a concert venue.

Nevertheless, the Doors wanted to show the packed house exactly what they could do. They turned up the sound and put on stellar performances. For three weeks, Jim engaged with fans at the front of the stage who could reach up and touch him or vice versa. In a review in *Variety*, a critic said the band "put on a hard-driving, earthy show," calling Morrison "an attraction in himself." *Village Voice* writer Richard Goldstein described how hot the Doors had become: "The Doors begin where the Rolling Stones leave off." Only months earlier the band was viewed by some as a Stones clone or rip-off; now they were being lauded for taking music to a new plane.

Although 1967 was the "Summer of Love," the Doors showed New York clubgoers that a different, darker future might be in store. Observers considered Morrison dangerous and unpredictable. This interpretation was reinforced by the extremes he seemed to personify, such as getting into a fistfight on stage at the club when Asher Dann, his own manager, tried to get him to stop swinging the mic in the packed venue because of the liability issue if he seriously hurt someone.

While the Scene closed during the Monterey Pop Festival, the band traveled to Long Island to play the Action House, a large industrial-looking club that had become the area's top live-music venue. The suburban Long Island spot had become cool, hosting Andy Warhol, Timothy Leary as well as the Velvet Underground and other bands associated with hip Manhattan. Allegedly owned by mobsters (with connections to Henry Hill, played by Ray Liotta in *Goodfellas*), mountains of money flowed in and out of the place and it became a must-play stop for the era's biggest names, including the Who, Cream, and Sly & the Family Stone. When tickets sold out, crowds gathered in the parking lot to party and blow off steam.

Jim reacted to the Doors being left out of the Monterey lineup in typical Morrison fashion, asking the bartender to line up multiple shots of Jack Daniels just before the band was scheduled to perform. He slugged them in order, leaving the shot glasses behind like little dead soldiers in his wake. Later, at a break, he performed the feat again, downing several more. Jumping back on stage, Morrison was nearly comatose. Too drunk to do much else, he began taking his clothes off. Ray, Robby, and John wisely shut down the performance, with roadie Bill Siddon hustling Jim backstage before he went too far in his impromptu strip show. He soon passed out.

The next night at the Action House had almost zero action. Morrison nursed a mammoth hangover. The show began and Jim could do nothing but groan into the microphone. After a few minutes, the other Doors helped him off stage. The show ended, but the party raged on at the Long Island establishment.

During the Doors' extended New York residency at the Scene, "Light My Fire" blasted into the top ten on the national singles charts, but Jim showed signs of cracking under the pressure. His fame grew exponentially while his flame burnt nonstop. The NYC shows brought out stars who just wanted to be around him, from Warhol and his entourage to Paul Newman, who wanted to work with Jim on a film soundtrack and talk to him about acting. Actor Tom Baker, destined to become one of Morrison's drinking buddies and on-again-off-again friend, exclaimed: "His performance was a classic one, giving off glimpses of all our beautiful tragic/comic American heroes . . . one moment I saw Brando's 'wild one,' the next James Dean's 'rebel,' then Chet Baker, and finally Elvis."

On the strength of the eerie, compelling "Light My Fire" and his angelic–demonic persona, Jim was becoming America's next big thing.

Journalist—and soon-to-be prolific novelist—Tom Robbins claimed to find his voice after seeing the Doors and writing an off-the-wall review of Morrison and the band. Robbins, in a state of ecstasy and exuberance, explained:

Their style is early cunnilingual, late patricidal, lunchtime in the Everglades, Black Forest blood sausage on electrified bread, Jean Genet up a totem pole, artists at the barricades, Edgar Alien Poe drowning in his birdbath, Massacre of the Innocents, tarantella of the satyrs, LA pagans drawing down the moon. . . . Musical equivalent of a ritual sacrifice, an amplified sex throb, a wounded yet somehow elegant yowl for the lost soul of America, histrionic tricksters making hard cider of the apples of Eden and petting the head of the Snake.

Robbins praised each member of the band for their contribution to a form of music that came from the intersection of the Sixties and the bowels of music history—an infusion of blues anguish, Dylanesque lyrics, and a stripped-down yet powerful dynamic that wiped away everything you had ever heard before. There was no mistaking the Doors. You knew it on the first note, with your body electrified and your brain on fire.

What Robbins grasped was the power and sanctity of the trio behind Morrison, but also that the full quartet hoisted the sound into holy territory. For him, Densmore was "perhaps the best drummer in all rock." Ray stood as "grandiose as the richest Baroque." While Krieger "explodes into startling new disclosures of chord and modulation." And Jim, Robbins explained, "begins where Mick Jagger and Eric Burden stop." Not only was the singer an "angel," but at the same time "a dog in heat" and "sexual in an almost psychopathic way."

The Doors from the start seized the rippling current running through the Sixties, sucking in the joy and the darkness and spitting it out at audiences in a way that left listeners jubilant with the promise of good and bad, light and evil.

In our historical memory, the Summer of Love provokes images of hippies and jam bands playing in fields for hundreds or thousands of fans. They are mellowed out on the vibe, the smell of grass is pervasive, and smoke billows toward the heavens, mixing with the fun-loving tunes. Yet the song of that summer was "Light My Fire," with its imagery of youthful, burning love and the power that it has to destroy.

If the music pushed you hypnotically toward the edge of a cliff, Morrison stood ready to push. But you also felt that he was ready to jump too, plunging into worlds and universes unknown.

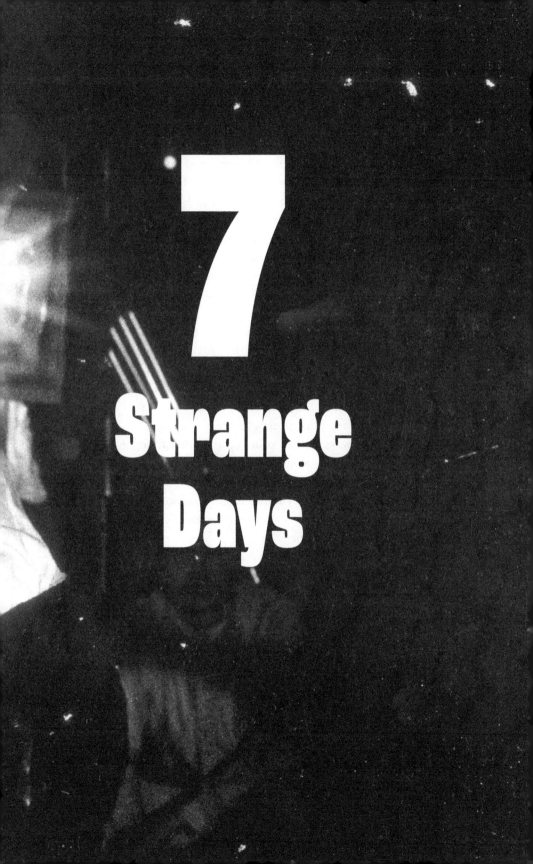

7

Strange Days

O n November 5, 1967, the new *Billboard* list of top-selling albums had the Doors' self-titled debut sitting at number three. Their latest release, *Strange Days*, had climbed to number four. Having two albums in the top five at the same time was Beatles territory and spoke to the band's widespread appeal. You would find Doors fans among the hippest of hippies, but at the same time Morrison was a heartthrob for teenage girls. *16* magazine had recently named him "one of the up-and-coming stars."

Fans snapped up *Strange Days* faster than Elektra execs had anticipated, totally different from the slow-growth sales of the debut. Two weeks earlier, journalists had reported that the record label received more than 350,000 advance orders. Others thought the preorders had topped half a million.

Journalist Bob Micklin had figured out the band's formula for success, calling them "the inheritors, and the advancers, of the brief legacy of contemporary message music established by the Beatles, Rolling Stones, Bob Dylan, and Donovan." What was at the core of this "message music" sweeping the nation? "An uneven mixture of blues, rock 'n' roll, existential philosophy, imagistic poetry, and pure electronic sound."

The Doors were a band your older brother thought was cool, while your kid sister sang along with the pop tunes and thought Jim was dreamy. "Light My Fire" had expanded the fan base, bringing the band to the masses. Some older fans and critics grumbled, as they always do when their favorites gain mainstream popularity. Success always brings criticism from some corners.

It is important to remember that while their first two records sat near the top of the charts, the band had only existed for a little over two years. The relentless work to craft the sound, followed by an exhaustive touring schedule, helped them get what they had hoped to achieve, but the accomplishments brought out hidden fissures that the media poked at. Reporters suddenly wanted to get inside, to know how they had done it, not just what they had achieved.

The way the band members answered these types of questions was telling. Robby emphasized the sanctity of the unit: "Our songs are credited to the group and there hasn't been the kind of ego problems some bands have where the lead singer or the guitar player wants to be the star." In this answer it seems Krieger was signaling that these were challenges the

Doors faced. Despite his laid-back personality, Robby was the youngest Door and the band-of-brothers mentality was important to him.

John and Ray responded to the backlash that came with popularity. In his typically direct fashion, Densmore explained, "A lot of people get shook about other people becoming successful." Manzarek scoffed at the idea that the band had to have a single type of fan, saying, "We're really against that sort of thing, like Us against Them, the Squares against the Hippies. Our music is for everybody who wants to listen." That they had to respond to becoming popular must have been startling since at the beginning of the year they were calling radio stations and asking for "Break On Through" to be played so much that the deejays on the other end knew it was them.

When 1967 began, they had been strictly an LA band with a record deal. The Whisky residency had brought them a taste of stardom, but, according to Robby, they were still "playing high school auditoriums and teen centers and skating rinks and American Legion halls." Success could have slipped away, as it had had for many rock groups. They didn't even have to look far for an example—Arthur Lee, who had urged Jac Holzman to sign the Doors, never broke through on a national level.

Like the Rolling Stones with "Satisfaction," "Light My Fire" changed everything for the Doors. "For the first half of the year, we were touring in a van as unproven unknowns," Krieger recalled. "For the second half, we were being flown to headlining gigs as number one artists."

In less than twelve months, the Doors had become America's top band.

Just four months after their debut album was released, the band was back in Sunset Sound studios. Their first sessions took place in May 1967, before the first album took off. That respite may have seemed like a break to them, but it didn't last long.

"Light My Fire" marched toward the top of the singles charts, and the resultant popularity sparked a frenzy. Life for the Doors became a vortex of concert dates, appearances, and constant travel.

They couldn't hole up in the studio and craft the next album. Instead, they would have to work around all their other commitments. This experience would be unlike the whirlwind of creativity that marked the debut.

With *The Doors* album, the idea was to get the live sound on tape as quickly as possible. This time around there was added pressure—not only from critics but from Elektra and themselves. How do you top an album that many were calling a masterpiece?

The technicalities fell to the team supporting the band, producer Paul Rothchild and engineer Bruce Botnick. In fact, Rothchild was so critical in crafting the band's sound that people started calling him "the fifth Door" (like the press had with the Beatles and George Martin). He and Botnick installed a state-of-the-art eight-track recording system and played around with new instruments, like the Moog synthesizer. The equipment gave the creative team more channels to fill and options when it came to maximizing the band's sound—making it fuller and more powerful.

Among the outside pressures the Doors felt was the imminent release of *Sgt. Pepper's Lonely Hearts Club Band*. Botnick had allegedly scored a pre-release copy of the album and the Beatles' song floored Jim, Ray, Robby, and John. *Sgt. Pepper's* had everything that Rothchild and the guys hoped to achieve, from brilliant songwriting to experimental sounds to using the latest technological innovations.

Just like the Rolling Stones with *Their Satanic Majesties Request*—and seemingly every other high-profile band in the world—the Beatles were charting a path that others felt they had to follow. Robert Fripp, the guitarist of King Crimson, summed up the reaction, saying, "After hearing *Sgt. Pepper*, my life was never the same again." The Doors pushed their limits to infuse some Beatles spirit into the recording sessions. From the way a band looked at cover art to how they thought about building an entire record that centered on a theme, *Sgt. Pepper's* influence ran deep.

Speaking about where the Doors were musically in those chaotic months, Manzarek explained, "What the musician is doing should be a complete delight to himself. Otherwise, what is the sense of doing it? If you are not knocked out by every note that you play, then something is wrong. On both our albums, for us, the bells are constantly ringing." Rothchild took something different from *Sgt. Pepper's*—the value of creating a full-bodied sound that was enhanced or improved by technology.

The Beatles had showed the world that they could release an album that captured the aura of the times. Yet *Sgt. Pepper's* and their follow-up, *The White Album* (1968), also drew from other performers and bands who were influencing the music scene, which leads to the question: Did the Doors influence the Beatles too? The dark, deeply personal songs on the Doors' debut album proved that there was a different, seedier side of the Summer of Love, which must have turned on Paul McCartney, the true dark heart of the Beatles.

In the swirl of the Sixties, it is difficult to determine precisely what took place, unless a musician said so publicly. In such a creative time, many were experiencing the same influences simultaneously. There was no mistaking the public's reaction, however: *Sgt. Pepper* held the top spot on the album chart from July to October of 1967.

At the beginning of that run, *Time* published a story on the hippies, which they identified as some three hundred thousand young people between seventeen and twenty-five years old. Most were upper-middle class and well-educated, but they were antiestablishment and advocated a "subversion of Western society" through nonviolence and the example they hoped to create. The Doors as people may have leaned hippie in thinking and action, but most of their music was from a different perspective and ran counter to what the majority of hippies preached.

With the Doors on the road to support the first album and "Light My Fire" about to explode into the national subconscious, new songs were being reworked, and some of the ones left off the first album were being polished. The influence of the Beatles, the Rolling Stones, Bob Dylan, and other bands may have come through most pointedly in what the Doors were not—a group representative of peace and love and hippie idealism. Instead, they were thrilling and chilling fans at shows and on their singles and albums. The allure was rooted in what other performers couldn't replicate: a combination of Jim's satanic poet-prince persona and the pounding psychedelic sound the band created.

The singer transformed when he got on stage, according to people who met him during their run of shows in 1967. Bill Siddons, later the band's manager, remembered: "I wasn't affected . . . meeting him, but when I saw him on stage I was more emotionally gripped and moved and disturbed than I had ever been at any similar type of thing." Summing up the experience, Siddons explained, "So what was my first impression of Jim? He scared me to death."

This fitful experience of engaging with the Doors was where the band diverged from their peers. You might experience a lot of emotions when seeing the Beatles, but you weren't scared. Similarly, even though the Stones were considered music's bad boys, their music was pretty straightforward, blues-infused rock and roll. A year later, Mick would sing from the viewpoint of the devil, but the listener took that idea only as far as they chose to. In contrast, Morrison personified malevolence.

The challenge for all singers, according to jazz vocalist Elizabeth Bougerol of the Hot Sardines, is that "singing and performing for a live audience are really two different things. Singing can at times be incredibly inwardly focused: You're concentrating on hitting that Venn diagram of control (accessing technique) and abandon (accessing emotion)." Performing in front of an audience—especially in a large auditorium—changes things: "Adding the crowd adds a huge, unpredictable element, and your goal is to make every single person feel the same emotion you feel. Often that means accessing feelings they keep locked away in their daily lives. If you can connect with them, you can bring them with you."

About Morrison, she added: "You hear [him] doing that in the live recordings, it's astonishing. You can hear the crowd following where he leads."

The Doors accentuated their defiant stance with aggressive psychedelic jams. Journalist Hank Zevallos described the opening of a Doors show:

Girls press forward against the stage. Morrison grunts, begins squirming, singing, and there's another barrage of flash bulbs and press towards the stage. The music weaves and screams into one climax after another. Morrison is literally raping the microphone between his quivering thighs, advancing toward the hungry girls pressing against the stage.

The mix of fear and sexual excitement can't be contained. Zevallos watched the scene in awe: "Few are frightened, most of them have eyes that mirror an erotic spell. And Morrison jumps hard among the fallen stand. . . . Shouting the lyrics. Screaming. You look at the girls and you swear they're having an orgasm."

In August, the Doors got back in the studio to record *Strange Days*, the title they had decided on after running through several alternatives. Jim's time on the road and the power of their newfound success had made him more confident, but also brazen. He missed some recording sessions altogether and showed up to others completely wasted. When he was there, Morrison recorded vocals in a tiny room in the Sunset Sound studio, which one journalist called "his dark little room." The eight-track deck gave the band more room to maneuver, ultimately adding nuance and depth to what they had achieved on the debut. Ray called the innovation "our plunge into the laboratory . . . we were mad scientists manipulating the aural spectrum for our diabolical creations . . . just sonic creativity." For example, they used the synthesizer to give Jim a haunting, full-bodied electronic amplification on the title track.

Some of the moves were less technology-based and just logical steps to get a bigger sound, like inviting bassist Doug Lubahn from the band Clear Light into the sessions. Ray showed him the bass notes and then Lubahn put his own sound on them. Watching the band record "You're Lost Little Girl," Hank Zevallos summed up the process as "one beautiful musical experience."

In a year of stunning debut albums from the likes of Jimi Hendrix, Pink Floyd, the Grateful Dead, and Janis Joplin with Big Brother and the Holding Company, the Doors had scored a number one single and dropped their second album in late September.

Sonically, *Strange Days* deepened the band's commitment to dark, brooding, and sexual psychedelic music. If America was caught up in a revolutionary spirit, its heartbeat was the Doors' first two records. In his dizzying explanation of the album's origins, Jim said:

It's more cleansing, purifying. You go through a realm of cares and despond, darkness, and madness, and it builds to an unendurable climax and returns to peace and order. Somehow it's a more stable order because you've gone through the whole other region.

According to journalist Mary Campbell of the Associated Press, *Strange Days* offered listeners influences from blues, jazz, and classical music, yet it also pulled "from the dark side" and was "on the literary side." She rightly predicted that the record would be "big with the public."

In his running sound-bite patter, Ray summed up the new sound in two words: "electric eclectic."

Fans and critics expected the Doors to follow up their debut album with more hits like "Light My Fire." When they didn't get the same sound on *Strange Days*, they searched for new ways to describe the album but were tempered in their assessment. "*Strange Days* is a better work for the group as a whole, as the men sound much tighter than they did on the first one," said Rory O'Connor, in a tepid review. "Each person is brought out more as an individual musician, improvisation being a major part of the Doors' talent."

In late 1967, journalist Beth Gillin also proved lukewarm. She focused on the aura of the band, which she labeled "frightening decadence" based on a "a sex-death-mysticism formula." The downfall, however, was Morrison, whose voice she described as "raw, terrifying, weirdly pure," but also "lacking range and force."

Her turn of phrase made for an interesting interpretation of the songs, explaining: "'You're Lost Little Girl' recalls Edith Piaf or Marlene Dietrich." Meanwhile, "People Are Strange" "has a melancholy, depression-Europe quality, with overtones of Brecht and Weill." What she determined is that, "Up to this point, the Doors have been dissecting the universe. They have found it putrefied," yet the screamed lyric of wanting the world "now" created a solution to the decay. Music was the answer and humanity's only hope.

Morrison saw *Strange Days* as innovative both lyrically and musically. "We expanded the song form by using plot, the spoken voice as an instrument, and sound effects," he explained. "Our first album was a blueprint of where we were going musically. The second album shows that we're partway there." Yet at the same time the album included poems and lyrics pulled from his earliest writings, including "Moonlight Drive," which he had sung to Ray on the beach two years earlier. Even then, however, there was a twist in that seemingly straightforward love song. In the song's final moments, the narrator warns that the lovers will drive down to the ocean and eventually "drown tonight." It's unclear if he's a murderer and has lured "baby" to this ignoble end or if it's some kind of murder–suicide pact. Perhaps it's all a metaphor for love and that all love eventually leads to death, despite its sincerity and depth—even as deep as the ocean or as bright as the moonlight.

Where the Doors intersected with hippiedom was on "When the Music's Over," another epic in the vein of "The End" but much more outward looking than the Oedipal masterpiece. The logical call to snap the lights off after the show, worked over and over again by Morrison and the band, transformed into a plea to save the world from the fires that humans had lit through wanton and destructive abuse of the planet.

There are two possible origins of the butterfly's scream that Jim demands in the middle of the song. One might be the 1965 noir film by the same name, a campy thriller "For Adults Only." The movie poster declared: "No one could satisfy her. . . . She lured them with her beauty and destroyed them with her sex." The *marry a rich dupe, kill him for money* flick spun on some unusually racy gay themes for that era. In December 1965, *Scream of the Butterfly* was playing at the 650-seat Apollo Arts Theater, located at Hollywood and Western, which specialized in foreign films.

The phrase may have also come from Alexander Pope's quote, "Who breaks a butterfly on a wheel," the line used by editor William Rees-Mogg in *The Times* that raised public outrage in Britain regarding the judicial sentences for Mick Jagger and Keith Richards after the Redlands drug bust. Certainly, Jim would have been paying attention and may have added the line since the arrests happened around the same time.

The most famous stanza of "When the Music's Over," however, is the awakening for "our fair sister," the earth. With a vengeance, Jim chanted the words in a singsong, rap fashion, spitting out what people had done to already ravage and destroy the purity of the planet. His response is a warning cry to the defilers that the young will take the earth back, inspired by the healing power of music. "Now!"

In October, on a trip back to Steve Paul's Scene in New York to promote the new album, the mix of theatrics and musicality was on Jim's mind. Backstage, he touted that the band was "much better in person," in contrast to the records, which only presented "a map of our work." His goal, he claimed, was to just sit down and talk to the audience rather than perform. Seeing the mysticism in the live show, Ray explained in language indicative of the era: "Our music short-circuits the conscious mind and allows the subconscious to flow free." The reviews of the shows, however, emphasized the "theater" quality of the band's performance, which produced "hot, electric thunder."

Incidentally, that trip across the country to New York led to one of the most important moments in Jim Morrison–mythmaking—the photo shoot with 16 magazine editor Gloria Stavers. One of the first women rock journalists, she played a large role in who became a star (or bigger star), based on the hold she had over a million teenage girls who bought the publication (and many more who got it secondhand from their friends).

Each new issue was like an event for the twelve-to-eighteen set that drove so much spending in the late Sixties. Every consumer product maker wanted the secret formula to unlocking that demographic. Stavers had figured it out—celebrity, beauty, and sex. Reportedly she received about three hundred letters a day from her readers, which provided a kind of inside look into the minds of her audience, quite similar to the way Stan Lee at Marvel got a massive amount of fan mail and read it dutifully to gain insight. Gloria's credibility was in part based on the boost she provided in launching the Beatles in America.

The famous photo shoot included the whole band, but, after some time, the guys left, and Jim stayed behind. There were rumors the two had become lovers and she wanted to capture him alone. Morrison realized the significance of the shoot and followed her closely around the studio, trying on things from her closet and striking seductive poses. Gloria captured Jim at his seductive best, staring directly into the camera in a leather shirt or wrapped in her long fur jacket. He looked angelic, confident, and—in some instances—slightly evil or deranged.

In the November profile, Stavers wrote as if introducing Morrison to the teen audience. "He is so whole, so complete, so all himself and nobody or nothing else that just meeting him is an unforgettable experience," she gushed in near-perfect teen speak. "Hearing him sing and watching him perform—well, that's really magic!" Stavers then proceeded to narrate what it was like to see the band perform live. Her description of Jim transformed him into angel and demon, but oozing sexuality:

And you feel something you have never felt before. It's like an electric shock that goes all through you. Jim is singing and you realize that it's a combination of him, the way he looks and moves, and his sound that has completely turned you on. His voice is like spirals of flame, and beautiful red and yellow colors seem to fly out of his fingertips.

Not only did Morrison set the reader on fire, but Stavers explained that the experience was unforgettable. In her mind, seeing Jim onstage was life changing: "you will never be the same again."

Given the prestige and public interest in the band on their trip east, Jim also posed for photographer Joel Brodsky, who had done a lot of work with the Doors, including the back cover of their debut record and the surrealist cover of *Strange Days*. He remembered that the band was smart about the value of imagery, explaining, "They had a visual orientation and seemed to understand the potential of a good photo session." After he took some individual photos, he let the guys go, so they didn't have to wait around. Again, Jim stayed behind.

According to Brodsky, the singer was drunk and stumbled around a bit. Shirtless and wearing a necklace he pilfered from Stavers, he raised his arms out in a crucifix pose and stalked around the room as best he could in a drunken haze. Smoldering and looking directly at the camera, Morrison's stint was dubbed the "young lion" session based on Jim's perfectly coiffed hair.

A week after the shoot, one of Brodsky's pics ran in *Village Voice*. The image set off a firestorm of requests for copies. The photographer said "like ten thousand." The young lion session seemed like a perfect moment in time, and a great artist was there to capture Jim at his best. "Morrison never really looked that way again," Brodsky said later. "Those pictures have become a big part of the Doors' legend. I think I got him at his peak."

Morrison the rock god was born.

Strange Days did not produce a number one single, but the two albums put the Doors in rarefied air—both achieved gold-record status. Rothchild summed up the collective thinking about the album, at least internally, saying, "We all thought it was the best album."

8
New Haven

POLICE DE[
NEW HAVEN C[
23750

Politics and crime were the lead stories in most major American newspapers on Monday, December 11, 1967. The previous evening Jacqueline Kennedy had made her first political appearance since her husband's assassination, arriving with much fanfare at a New York State Democratic fundraising dinner costing five hundred dollars a plate. Other noteworthy guests included future 1968 presidential candidates Robert F. Kennedy and Eugene J. McCarthy, as well as Edward M. Kennedy. RFK joked that the event might as well serve as "the Kennedy Christmas party."

Yuletide festivities were on many people's minds as the holiday approached. Others, though, were caught up in the hoopla surrounding Lyndon B. Johnson's daughter Lynda Bird marrying Marine Captain Charles S. Robb in the East Wing of the White House in Washington, DC, the previous weekend. The high-profile event gave the president the opportunity to downplay the activists protesting the war in Vietnam, explaining that the young people leading demonstrations were simply a "few exhibitionists . . . definitely in the minority." Yet at his daughter's wedding and reception, police were on hand to keep a small crowd of protesters away from the event.

With the intensity of the antiwar protests, ongoing civil rights campaigns, and the growing concern about drug use among young people, few could ignore the public release of a report by the FBI that revealed "serious crime" in America had "skyrocketed" in 1967, up 16 percent over the previous year. The most chilling statistic for most readers was the fact that violent crimes in the suburbs—usually considered safer than other places—was growing at a rate faster than in the nation's large metro cities. The national rate for murders also mirrored the overall figure at 16 percent. As a result, both the president and FBI Director J. Edgar Hoover demanded that Congress provide additional funds to battle what they viewed as a crime wave sweeping the nation.

Many Americans conflated rising violent crime rates with drug use by hippies. An investigation into the "drug scene" in Boston published that same day by journalist Robert L. Levey claimed: "There is one generalization that applies to all the types in the hippie underground of Boston and Cambridge. They have experimented with drugs." The story included tales of college students selling marijuana and LSD imported from San Francisco and New York and young teen runaways who were caught up in the scene.

For Captain Joseph Jordan of the Boston narcotics squad, the hippie influence was not about love and peace, but its detrimental effect on younger teens. He likened hippies to "wolves masquerading as sheep. They throw out a lot of propaganda that just isn't true." Representing the thinking of much of the establishment, Jordan complained, "The hippies live in a complete drug atmosphere. Their whole environment deals with drugs." Although law enforcement agents pinpointed marijuana for its widespread use, what they really feared was a growing epidemic of amphetamines ("speed"), particularly the form injected by needle directly into the user's vein.

According to Levey, though, LSD reigned as the kingpin of hippie drugs: "The official initiation to the hippie underground." One of the young people he interviewed described his first acid trip as an "incredible state of harmony and love." Another claimed the drug "just opens your head to such huge vistas." Yet Levey relayed that the hippies knew that some people had life-threatening reactions to LSD, explaining that one young woman's sister had been hospitalized for two months after a bad dose. The reporter summed up the drug scene like many in the "straight" world might, saying, "Some can handle it—for others it is a seductive and destructive course."

A thread tying together these disparate events and stories was another piece of news reported that day and over the next week: the arrest of Jim Morrison late Saturday night while on stage in New Haven, Connecticut. Perhaps not compelling enough to make it to the front page of the conservative mainstream media, the singer's arrest and the resulting fallout held different meanings depending on where one stood on the current-event spectrum.

Speaking with a woman who was seventeen years old when Morrison was arrested on stage by the New Haven police force, I asked if she were a Doors fan back then. Her answer, with hesitancy in her voice as if she were instantly reliving the era: "Oh no! That was druggy music." For her, the music scene at the time centered on the Beatles—the wholesome, *Ed Sullivan Show* "I Want to Hold Your Hand" version, not the mind-altered, questioning-authority band of the late Sixties.

The one-word label—"druggy"—for the Doors is significant in how it becomes both a moniker and a definition. Remember, December 1967 is five months *after* the band had hit the top of the charts with "Light My

Fire" and three months *after* their national appearance on the *Ed Sullivan Show*. The idea that Doors fans were either hard-core rock-psychedelic enthusiasts or teenyboppers who had Morrison pinups on their walls is more nuanced. Some longtime fans were in many respects turned off by the band's mainstream success. Newer listeners probably looked past the bad-boy image and the drug overtones.

What we know for sure is that the parents of these Doors fans and others in the older generations who were in authority positions resented the threat the band and others like them epitomized. It seems to be over the top to look back and consider a rock group a *danger*, but, since Elvis Presley's explosion into the national consciousness in the 1950s, popular figures in music were seen as potentially threatening. The Doors challenged the ideals such people held dear. In this specific case, then, the band becomes a critical lens in examining how society and those in power come to grips with detractors or other critics outside what they consider the norm.

The nation was on edge that fall because of the late October antiwar protest held at the Lincoln Memorial where some seventy thousand activists, hippies, war vets, Black Power members, and others gathered to show Lyndon Johnson how they felt about the war in Southeast Asia. After several speakers addressed the masses, including writer Norman Mailer and child psychologist Benjamin Spock, the crowd crossed the Potomac River toward the Pentagon. Johnson railed against the "irresponsible acts of violence and lawlessness by many of the demonstrators," but there were just one thousand arrests and no felonies. If anything, the crowds were tame and reacted primarily against the aggression of the police and military that arrested them. The eyewitness accounts of the brutality—particularly on women protestors—were shocking.

The march pointed to a sea change in thinking, but also put the nation even more into us-versus-them camps. "For the first time in history," explained historian Thomas Heinrich, "Americans from all walks of life rose up in mass protest against US military intervention."

The viciousness of the police response to the march on the Pentagon, according to Mailer, was essential to his concept that "the center of American might be insane." Similar to the old adage that insanity meant doing the same thing twice and expecting a different outcome, Mailer determined people were "caught in an unseen vise whose pressure could split their mind from their soul." In his aggressive, resolute fashion, the novelist connected the "schizophrenia" of capitalism, technology, and religion to the war. "America needed the war," Mailer explained in *The Armies of the Night.* "It would need a war so long as technology expanded . . . and the cities and corporations spread like cancer; the good Christian Americans needed the war or they would lose their Christ."

So while Baby Boomers and others looking back from the twenty-first century might layer much of the 1960s with feelings of nostalgia or longing for the ideals they may have believed in at the time, we must never forget that the "Summer of Love" was only joyous for *some* of the people, *some* of the time. For others, the 1960s would be an era of repression, inequality, exclusion, and heartbreak. Dread and fear served as the undercurrent pulsing through the age. The challenge was that Mailer's description of national psychosis was largely undetected by those it afflicted. Yet it was at the heart of why the state would react so definitively to repress an artist like Morrison.

Jim's arrest in December 1967 while on stage at the New Haven Arena is important in understanding the decade. The incident represents how myriad people and institutions in a position of power were willing to use their authority to stamp out or thwart those who symbolized something they didn't understand or even attempt to comprehend. For those wielding a hammer, as is said, everything looks like a nail. The establishment's reaction to Morrison and the Doors was to look at them as something evil that had to be stopped.

Is the New Haven incident and Morrison's onstage arrest part of the singer's mythology? Certainly, but it's more than simply iconography or yet another aspect of his life blown out of proportion. For every person who believed in the potential of the Sixties as the dawn of a better age, there were many more who saw the era as threatening, immoral, and—perhaps most important—antithetical to what the United States epitomized.

The FBI crime report provided real-world evidence for what many people were feeling—that young people and drugs had set the nation on a path careening toward anarchy. But they didn't necessarily need an FBI document to reinforce what they saw when they looked out their windows or viewed the evening news. For millions, those who Richard Nixon would later call "the silent majority," the Summer of Love was a summer of madness.

As the hottest band in the land, the Doors became more than just another rock band; they embodied darkness, violence, and the fear of psychedelic drug use. The band members themselves could sense this vibe.

When the Doors got into Middle America, outside of their home base of LA, San Francisco, and other cosmopolitan meccas on the East Coast, the way people viewed them changed quickly. "Diners in Ohio called us fags for wearing long hair," Densmore explained. Jim, however, really riled the crowds, the media, and the local police. "Morrison was devastating in those days," remembered the drummer. "He wore his leather pants twenty-four hours a day and looked like some kind of swamp lizard out on the border."

For Morrison, his public persona bolstered his deeply held belief that all authority needed a thumb directly in the eye socket. Is it any wonder that the son of a future Navy admiral would have antiauthority issues? For Jim, resistance was personal and he was a no-holds-barred provocateur. The police were no exception, even the small-town ones who saw him as the devil and might beat him up if given the chance. Morrison didn't back down, even when his own safety was on the line.

The scene: December 9, 1967, the day after Jim Morrison's twenty-fourth birthday. The Doors are scheduled to play a show at the New Haven Arena, filled with two thousand screaming fans, just a handful of blocks from the campus of Yale University. Thirty or thirty-five police officers are on duty, searching the arena for people who entered unlawfully.

Backstage in an empty shower stall, just beyond the band's dressing room. Jim and an eighteen-year-old student from Southern Connecticut State University are talking and kissing. A police officer patrolling the area investigates, after someone allegedly reported that two people were having sex somewhere in the depths of the arena.

Police Officer: "Vacate the area."

Morrison: "Eat it."

Police Officer (raising a black aerosol can of mace shoulder high): "Last chance!"

Morrison: "Last chance to eat it."

The police officer sprays Jim in the face and douses the student in the toxic wash. Jim allegedly "scuffles" with the officer and screams out in pain. Blinded for several minutes, his screams alert the rest of the band and their entourage, including then road manager Bill Siddons. While the cops try to throw the singer in the back of a paddy wagon, the band intervenes and tells the nearby officers that the person they just doused with mace is the reason two thousand fans are packed into the arena. They are supposed to take the stage, not get their lead singer medical attention.

The arresting officers and their commander, Lieutenant James P. Kelly, head of the Youth Division of the New Haven Police Department, relent and let Jim go, fearing a riot if they tell the crowd that the concert is cancelled. One stipulation is that Morrison and the officer who maced him must shake hands and apologize to each other. For his part, the cop admits that he had no idea who Morrison was when he demanded that he leave the shower area.

In the years since New Haven, some eyewitnesses allege that Morrison was supposed to surrender to the police after the show and that Kelly ordered him to "act properly." In any case, it took nearly an hour for the effects of the mace to wear off. According to Manzarek, "a doctor had to attend to him and the girl and flush their eyes with a saline solution." Jim coughed violently as he attempted to expel the spray.

The two thousand people in the crowd had no idea what had just happened backstage. All they knew was that the two opening acts were long done and they wanted the Doors. Seconds ticked into minutes; it was eventually an hour before the band emerged. The spectators roared to life when they got their first glimpse of the famed Lizard King decked out in a dark shirt, dark jacket, and skintight leather pants. He strutted back and forth with a wild, aggressive posture. Triggered by the mace incident, he was filled with rage.

The Doors launched into "Five to One," an ode to the rising power of young people and their desire to soon take society's reigns. Fred Powledge, covering the concert for *Life* magazine, watched Morrison stalk the stage. "He was dangerous," the reporter noted, "but danger was part of the show." Like the others in the New Haven audience that night, Powledge viewed Jim as "carnality" in the flesh. When Morrison screamed out the song's final lines "We want the world and we want it . . . NOW!" many in the crowd joined in, which gave added force to the hostility of the demand.

According to eyewitnesses at the New Haven show, Morrison was aggressive and maniacal. He pushed the heavy bottom of the microphone stand into the crowd, barely missing some young teenaged girls in the front row. The police responded, a writer said, "staring up at Morrison with undisguised hate." They then turned on "somebody's daughter" standing near the stage. She was "dragged by her scruff" by a cop, "twisted and turned like some little animal."

The band launched into "Back Door Man." Morrison finally broke. Unable to let the injustice stand any longer, he used a break in the lyrics to begin telling a little tale while the band kept pace behind him. "I want to tell you about something that happened just two minutes ago right here in New Haven," he began. "This is New Haven, Connecticut, United States of America?" The crowd quieted, not sure what was going on. Their ears perked when they heard their hometown mentioned.

"We weren't doing anything, you know," Morrison would explain. "Just standing there and talking. . . ."

Angry and hoping the crowd would turn on the police, he called the officer who maced him and his companion "a little blue man in a little blue cap." Pulling out the mace, which he likened to "shaving cream," Morrison told the crowd, "And then he squirts it in my face. . . . And I'm blind. . . . He blinds me." Then he brought the point home, emphasizing the "us-versus-them" message to the congregated masses: "I'm just like you guys . . . he did it to me, they'll do it to you." Expletives punctuated every sentence.

The cops lining the stage area visibly tensed as the singer swore and hurled additional insults their way. Fans began to stomp their feet on the arena's wooden floor, the sound amplifying the concerns of Kelly and the dozens of officers stationed in front of the stage area. Simultaneously, police alleged, they received complaints from the audience about Morrison's foul language. Already on edge, they had had enough.

The house lights went on, immediately illuminating the dark stage area and snapping thousands of fans to attention. Morrison's microphone was cut off. Lieutenant Kelly and Officer Wayne Thomas walked toward Jim as Ray moved from behind the keyboard and made his way to Morrison. He whispered in his ear. Krieger turned toward the officers with a scowl, as if he wanted to wish them away and hit his next note.

The two middle-aged, uniformed officers approached Morrison from opposite sides. Morrison, sensing the danger, raised the microphone to Lieutenant Kelly: "Say your thing, man!"

Two cops, one singer. One grabbed the microphone and declared the concert over. The other grabbed Jim around his upper arm. Looking at the footage more than half a century later, Morrison's reaction was to continue playing to the crowd. He made several odd, distorted faces as the police got closer, as if wondering what they were doing. Quickly they began to pull him from the stage.

Morrison's comic response only lasted a couple seconds, though, as both officers put their hands on him. In the surviving clip, you can see Jim visibly pull away and snap into a more defiant posture. The officers then dragged him toward the curtain behind them as many other cops nearby jumped onstage, preparing for the crowd's probable reaction after being wound up by Morrison. The phalanx of officers started pushing and shoving the crowd toward the exit doors.

Although the officers who pulled Jim from the stage seemed under control—kindly even—eyewitnesses reported a totally different scene backstage. Once removed from the eyes of two thousand witnesses, a group of police officers half-dragged, half-carried Morrison down steps that led to the parking lot. They treated him exactly as one would imagine a small-town police force would respond to rock music's dark prince in the late 1960s.

According to future road manager Vince Treanor, who saw the incident firsthand, two officers held Jim's arms, making it impossible for him to get away. "In front," Treanor recounted, "there was another cop actually punching and slapping him." They then dragged Morrison out to the awaiting patrol car. He fell as they tried to get him into the vehicle. After he hit the ground, they took turns kicking him while he was on the pavement. Finally, the officers relented and threw Jim in the back of the car.

When they suspected that *Life* magazine photographer Tim Page got most of the brutality on film, including five officers beating up a teenager, the cops arrested the journalist and researcher Yvonne Chabrier, as well as *Village Voice* music critic Michael Zwerin. The police tried to confiscate Page's camera and its contents. Defiantly, the photographer exclaimed: "You touch this film and I'll see you in the Supreme Court!" Despite his press credential and telling the arresting officer that he had spent time with the press corps in Vietnam, the cop roughly frisked Page and threatened to "bust him up" if he resisted being placed in the back of a wagon. According to Powledge, a handful of other concertgoers were also arrested.

There was no cooling-off period on the ride to the station at 165 Court Street for those arrested or the officers. Once inside the building, several cops harassed Morrison for having long hair, questioning whether he was a man or a woman. Used to these types of antagonistic jeers, Jim told them they were ugly and called them pigs. Upping the ante, one of the more belligerent officers told the singer that he'd give him a real beating once his shift ended.

The possibility of real bodily injury hung heavy in the dark, putrid cell, a drunk tank right out of the movies. The small space was dirty and had a rough-hewn wooden bench and a seatless toilet that filled the cramped area with an awful smell. Morrison's eyes were still irritated from the mace attack. But before Jim's threatening nemesis on the police payroll could get his revenge-laden hands on the singer, several members of the band's entourage, including Bill Siddons, showed up at the station and demanded Morrison be set free.

Morrison and the others were charged with indecent exhibition, breach of the peace, and resisting an officer. Siddons paid the $1,500 bail bond in the early morning hours of December 10. In his mug shot, Morrison was still angry, with a demonic look in his eyes. Several hours later, a crowd of teens and other protesters appeared outside the station, shouting for Morrison's release.

The police response was direct. In return for exercising their First Amendment rights in New Haven, nine additional activists were detained.

New Haven Police Close 'The Doors'
  —*New York Times*
4 Arrested at Rock Concert, Singer Is Dragged from Stage
  —*Hartford Courant*
Seize Singer & 3 At Rock Concert
  —*NY Daily News*

Initial newspaper reports of the New Haven fracas told a story that painted Morrison and the police as equally responsible for what unfolded that night. Reporters called the initial confrontation between Jim and the officer who maced him "a run-in with police," without stressing that the cop used a semi-lethal weapon against another human for simply being in the wrong place at the wrong time and (most likely) for looking like a hippie—imagine that—at a rock concert.

Reading some accounts, one would imagine a much different scene then the one that actually occurred. The brazen statement "a fight broke out," which then led to Jim's arrest, was completely out of context. Other reports called Morrison a "mangy-haired singer," clearly labeling him in an attempt to reinforce the difference between him and those on the proper side of polite society.

Surprisingly, journalists didn't even seem to rally to the injustice perpetrated on their colleagues—Page, Chabrier, or Zwerin—who were seemingly arrested for merely carrying out their journalistic duties.

Some onlookers did take a stand, however, and attempted to provide a fuller picture of the events that transpired. A few days after the bust, Yale art history professor Standish D. Lawder wrote a letter to the *Yale Daily News* defending Morrison: "There was no disturbance until the cops provided one."

Later, Manzarek put the entire incident into larger perspective, reiterating that it was the police who were "the only ones who rioted." What they did to Morrison was simply by any measure "a violation of his civil liberties and rights as a human being." Rather than serving justice, the police reacted to Jim's provocation in anger and then fed fuel to a fire that they themselves sparked.

Earlier that year Mick Jagger and Keith Richards were arrested at the guitarist's Redlands estate in West Sussex, England, and charged with drug possession after being under surveillance by local authorities and a British newspaper called the *News of the World*.

The incident, involving the famous Stones and a merry band of friends and partygoers, eventually set off an international debate over the role of the police, media, and the modern drug scene. At the time, however, Mick and Keith's main concern was staying out of jail. Both men were sentenced to extended jail time, though they immediately appealed the verdicts.

For the public, the glimpse inside the lives of Jagger and Richards was titillating and provided endless fodder for discussions about the lifestyles of the rich and famous. However, others questioned whether the jail sentences were too harsh and handed down precisely because of the iconic stature of the young musicians.

On July 1, conservative editor William Rees-Mogg wrote an op-ed in the *London Times* that outlined the folly of the arrest and questioned the legality of the sentencing, particularly Jagger's punitive punishment. The article played a significant role in changing British public opinion. On the last day of the month, the charges were overturned. For Mick and Keith, however, staring down jail time snapped them back to the reality of the lengths the establishment would go to rein in outsiders, particularly when drugs were involved.

The rock-and-roll lifestyle came under fire when tied so closely to drug use, rebellion, and anarchy. The Rolling Stones were pitched to the world as the anti-Beatles, a group of young hellions who epitomized the wild side. Their mix of loud rock music tinged with rhythm and blues— another trait shared with the Doors—provided the soundtrack for the global counterculture. For those in power, however, their revolution had to be quelled.

Looking back from the twenty-first century, it seems ludicrous to put drugs at the heart of a national or global scourge, particularly when young people were dying in Vietnam and Black Americans were being denied civil rights, but the Stones bust was just the first in a series of high-profile arrests. Over the next eighteen months, fellow Stones bandmate Brian Jones and Beatles George Harrison and John Lennon were also arrested.

The New Haven arrest brought 1967 to an end with a thud, so unlike where the band had been just several months earlier when "Light My Fire" was at the top of the charts. Yet it almost seemed logical in an era in which dissent had to be held in check. In this case, it was not the use of mace on an unarmed, unthreatening individual but the dangerous reaction *against* authority by someone who didn't look like the stereotypical boy next door.

Questioning authority was on people's minds. In December 1967, for example, just eleven days after Morrison's arrest, *The Graduate* opened at theaters across America. Based on the Charles Webb novel, the film starred Dustin Hoffman as Benjamin Braddock, a college grad who is lost between what polite society expects of him and the depravity he sees (and experiences) around him.

While the young man's illicit affair with Mrs. Robinson (played by Anne Bancroft), a longtime friend of his parents, shocked filmgoers, the battle between generations is at the heart of the film. The blatant attempt at selling youth and innocence to American audiences in such an overtly commercial film alienated some critics, but the film won Mike Nichols a Best Director Academy Award and the film was nominated in six other categories, including Best Picture, Best Actor, Best Actress, and Best Supporting Actress.

From any number of perspectives, violence was also foremost in the national consciousness. The Doors had created a musical ethos based on Morrison's long-held beliefs in the power of violence. Their sound thumped and thundered, reflecting their era and projecting it out to audiences who were unnerved by its energy—but simultaneously attracted to the pop sensibility that pushed album sales. Morrison knew what listeners wanted. As he had explained, "America was conceived in violence. Americans are attracted to violence. They attach themselves to processed violence, out of cans. They're TV-hypnotized . . . they're emotionally dead."

From the band's first encounters with the media and the publicity machine that would turn them into superstars, Jim courted darkness, an image that would set him apart. Brooding might have been his natural inclination, but does one amplify that trait cynically or simply live it? Morrison was certainly aware that he was creating a self to project onto the national scene. His persona was not aping his heroes Dylan, Sinatra, or Elvis. Morrison the rock god was wholly unique in his vision of who he should be and what fans desired (or feared they desired in their heart of hearts).

In his Elektra Records bio—more or less his introduction to the world—Jim proclaimed: "I've always been attracted to ideas that were about revolt against authority. . . . I like ideas about the breaking away or overthrowing of established order." Bluntly, he said, "revolt, disorder, chaos, especially activity that seems to have no meaning." The young singer equated these ideas to the "road to freedom."

While these words could be simply read as a slick attempt to create an image and aura for the fledgling band, in the mid-1960s they mirrored the throbbing national anxiety from a growing overseas war, civil unrest at home, and the post-traumatic stress of a president's murder. And it wasn't as if Jim were sitting idly home each night. He was in the spotlight and pushing the edges, probing for boundaries that were actually fluid if you were young, beautiful, and famous.

Looking back on the arrest decades later, Krieger discussed its consequences. "We became outlaw legends brimming with counterculture credibility. But we had also created an expectation of chaos." What Doors fans wanted—or seemed to demand—after the bedlam in New Haven was more. According to the guitarist, "The headline in *Life* summed up the road we were now on: 'Wicked Go the Doors.'"

New Haven proved Morrison's bona fides. He backed his anger and disgust with action. The Doors faced intense scrutiny from the forces that already distrusted hippie rock stars and their legions of fans. As a band, they were caught up in finding out if there were limits—and then exceeding them. "We enjoyed the idea of pushing limits, and it seemed like the crowds enjoyed it as much as we did," Robby explained. "If the crowd didn't riot, we felt like we hadn't done our job. And if the crowd didn't get a taste of New Haven, they felt like they didn't get their money's worth."

As musicians, pressing to achieve new heights meant something different to Ray, Robby, and John, something akin to achievement—a better solo, a longer jam, getting deeper into the vibe. Their aspirations centered on making better music, stronger ties to listeners, and unwrapping the mysticism of their instruments. For Jim, though, always the provocateur, the rush toward *more* meant consuming outrageous quantities of booze and drugs. Audiences watched his attempts at physically breaking on through—whether it was shaman-like dancing, leaping off the stage, or hurling his body into the floor—but it was the swirl of chemicals inside his body that would eventually become unsustainable.

Five months after his arrest alongside Morrison, Michael Zwerin wrote about the incident, but reading the article now there is an aura of the authentic Sixties unraveled in the piece that is irrefutable. He describes the feeling of snorting heroin with a friend, and then again later as he drove to New Haven (presumably with his friends and fellow journalists Page and Chabrier). When a police officer pulls them over at the Connecticut border for having Arizona plates, Zwerin declares that carrying pot or other drugs makes "routine brushes with the police . . . each a potential disaster." As a result, he declares a mantra for his generation—or at least those who regularly used or carried drugs: "All cops are enemies."

Walking to the show a little later, Zwerin noticed cops everywhere. "Cops walking to work in pairs swinging billy clubs. Dumb-looking cops. Burly cops with red faces. . . . All cops ready to defend the Republic against obscenity and hair." He described the officers guarding the stage that night as "serious and bitter." But the writer noticed Morrison's red eyes and took note of the singer's "freaking out," including "grinding, bumping, and coming close to swallowing the microphone." According to Zwerin, "If you had a dirty mind, you might call it obscene."

Obscenity was on the minds of the New Haven police—or at least used as a justification for arresting Jim. Would anyone really believe that people at a Doors show were so offended that they begged the cops to make the bad man on stage stop swearing?

Morrison wasn't targeted in the same way Jagger and Richards had been in the Redlands drug bust, but both episodes were the logical conclusion of traditional establishment backlash when dissenters pushed too far. The police in New Haven could not stand that Jim made them look bad in front of the local citizenry. When he defied their attempts at intimidation (which included packing the arena with nearly three dozen cops, verbal threats, and physical assault), they did what they could in the moment: kill the mic and shut down the show, despite the bedlam they unleashed among two thousand people who had no comprehension of what they were seeing. People were injured, arrested, property destroyed, and there were some who probably suffered from short- or long-term mental turmoil from the chaos. Yet the melee was unleashed by the defenders of public safety—civil liberties be damned.

New Haven matters because it represents yet another nail in Sixties idealism. No ground for compromise or cooperation existed between those in power and those who challenged their authority. Morrison's arrest, for example, alerted the authorities nationwide that this was someone who needed to be kept under observation. FBI agents opened a file on the singer and began collecting evidence. Jim was seen as a threat, which would have chilling consequences a little over a year later in Miami.

Whether based on residual anger or just as a practical joke, Jim later satirized the arrest in the song "Peace Frog" on *Morrison Hotel*: "Blood in the streets in the town of New Haven."

A month later, most of the charges against Morrison were dropped when he failed to appear in court (forfeiting the $1,500 bond), but he did pay a twenty-five-dollar fine for disturbing the peace. Ironically, the rickety New Haven Arena, for most of its existence a decrepit old hockey rink, was torn down in 1974. A new building on the site is now home to the city's FBI office.

9
Waiting for the Sun

Anyone who expected the New Haven arrest to slow down or change Jim Morrison would be proved wrong. As a chaotic world rolled into 1968, the Doors were arguably the most important rock band in the world, but Jim was out of control. He had just turned twenty-five and seemed hell-bent on collecting experiences, pushing himself and those around him to journey with him toward the unknown—exactly the kind of behavior *regular* society scorns.

Jim had never been to Las Vegas, the home of his hero Frank Sinatra. Vegas offered him yet another experience, but like so many Morrison tales, the experience quickly turned south. The outing was supposed to be a couples' trip with novelist Robert Gover and his girlfriend Beverly and Jim and Pamela Courson. Gover was a new friend who Jim admired for his dedication to writing. He had written the cult classic *One Hundred Dollar Misunderstanding*, a satirical examination of class, socioeconomic disparity, and race. It was January 28 and the foursome planned to go to dinner and a show, but, while prepping to leave, Jim and Pam got into an argument. She wouldn't go, so they left her in LA and headed east across the desert.

When Jim argued with Pam, he frequently would search for a way to release his anger, unbeknownst to those who might later get caught up in his wrath. That January night seemed an antidote, though, as the threesome enjoyed their trip and things remained subdued. But, as was the norm with Jim, it didn't last long.

They decided to go to the Pussycat A Go Go Casino to see a popular six-man singing group called Stark Naked and the Car Thieves. The Pussycat was a dance club and gambling house in the heart of the Strip. The establishment was considered an "it" locale, a place where the young, famous, and wealthy went to mix and mingle with Vegas showgirls and entertainers. The Pussycat logo featured a black cat and a scantily clad illustration of a woman half bent over in a somewhat seductive pose with little mice watching her.

A little before midnight, Jim, Bob, and Beverly walked toward the entrance, stopped by Paul Swogger and Vince Gardner, the club doormen. Morrison pretended he was smoking a doobie and flicked the cigarette onto the pavement near the club—typical Jim messing with people. Taking offense and not realizing that Jim was a celebrity, the bouncers exchanged words with Morrison, who—as usual—mouthed back, despite being outnumbered. One of the men pulled a billy club on the singer, allegedly hitting him on the head.

Jim's blood flowed and the chaos mounted, so Pussycat owner Robert Hirsch called the police. The cops arrived, took one look at Morrison, and arrested him. If one understands Vegas history, it would not be a stretch to imagine that the police force was in cahoots with club owners in these situations. A screaming and bloody Morrison is going to get taken to jail every time regardless of the circumstances, perhaps just for looking like a hippie. For good measure, they arrested Gover too, even though he was simply a bystander.

When confronted, Morrison always pushed back, so the arrest got worse. He called the cops every expletive imaginable, and they soon ran out of patience with the long-haired hippie. In an era before continuous media coverage, they didn't care who Morrison was outside of Clark County, Nevada. The charge was "drunk in public," but the real challenge was whether Jim would get out of Vegas unharmed. The more he screamed, the angrier the cops got.

In *No One Here Gets Out Alive,* the exchange with the police is more sinister—the cops heckled Jim and Bob and eventually strip-searched them to see if they were in fact men (after asserting they may just be "beautiful" girls). Just like in New Haven, several officers promised him a "date" outside after their shifts ended. Still, Jim didn't stop.

In his mug shot, Morrison looks a little drunk and confused, sporting stubble and dirty hair. There are no visible signs of the clubbing or marks on his face. Fortunately, Beverly was able to bail the two men out of jail before the next shift change, hustling Jim away from the station as fast as possible.

Apparently, Morrison had been drinking since ten in the morning, so the entire Vegas episode could be chalked up as just another drunken performance. The arrest could also be seen as a sign of where his life was headed. Jim had a major problem and no one to turn to for help. He was floating on a wave of alcohol unmindful of the dangers ahead.

As a matter of fact, Gover believed Morrison attracted turmoil naturally. The novelist explained: "His charisma was such that your ordinary upholder of the established order could be infuriated merely by the sight of Morrison strolling down the street." Jim had an intuitive aura, "that invisible something about him that silently suggested revolution, disorder, chaos." Perhaps, like America itself, Morrison just never saw it coming.

As 1968 unfolded, it became clear that it would be a watershed moment in history. For Jim, the line "no one here gets out alive" would take on new meaning—and might have even been in his mind that cold winter night in the desert.

The same day of Morrison's booking, newspapers in Nevada reported on a "small nuclear blast" set off by the Atomic Energy Commission one hundred miles northwest of Las Vegas. The test, which had occurred three days earlier, was part of the military's Project Plowshare, an attempt to find peaceful ways to use nuclear power for public good, like digging canals and highway passes through mountains, not just to blow up a future enemy.

A small nuclear bomb is of course still momentous. The explosion—equivalent to 2,500 tons of dynamite—threw rock, dirt, and debris 1,900 feet into the air, even though it was considered a "shallow detonation." The bomb carried a 2.3-kiloton payload, much smaller than the 13-kiloton bomb that the United States dropped on Hiroshima. There were no reports that Las Vegas hotels held watch parties, as they did in the Fifties when the Chamber of Commerce put out a calendar of detonations and the best places in town to watch them as a means of enticing tourists to "Atomic City." Some Vegas establishments even hosted "Dawn Bomb Parties," which began at midnight and featured all-night drinking and singing until the explosion lit up the dark sky.

With the war in Vietnam intensifying and persistent unrest from sea to shining sea, 1968 would be a year of murder, mayhem, and madness. From this vantage point, Morrison's arrest could have been viewed as an omen, just like the continued nuclear tests in the Nevada desert. As the year progressed, the number of tests increased to almost weekly explosions, the majority "weapons related."

"I'm interested in anything about revolt, disorder, chaos, especially activity that has no meaning. It seems to me to be the road to freedom."
　—Jim Morrison

A month later, the Doors reassembled to work on their third album *Waiting for the Sun*. Taking advantage of the technological advances in the music industry, they used a sixteen-track recording deck. Ray, Robby, John, and Jim were eager to work together in the studio. They tackled Morrison's long poem "The Celebration of the Lizard," which they believed would be one entire side of the album. Their progress was hampered by the technical skill necessary to orchestrate the piece. They weren't able to perfect the vibe that would have made the epic poem perfect.

By March, however, the enthusiasm began to wane. The first two albums had come together fairly quickly and were primarily songs the band had worked on countless times together in rehearsals and their early residencies. *Waiting for the Sun* was different because they were no longer brimming with material. And the expectations of their fans and Elektra had grown. The new album needed to produce hit singles to keep the band's momentum going. From the Beatles and Marvin Gaye to Canned Heat and Jimi Hendrix, there was no shortage of performers gunning for the Doors.

At the same time Paul Rothchild applied added strain by letting loose his perfectionist tendencies. For each track, the producer demanded extra takes, which frustrated Ray, Robby, and John. Some songs exceed a hundred takes. Nerves were so frayed that John hit his limit, quit, but then returned the next day. In the meantime, as time frittered away, Jim alternatively arrived late, was bored with the process, or was knockdown drunk (sometimes all three).

No one was happy with the singer's mini rebellion, which was fueled by the fact that they couldn't get "Celebration" down and eventually gave up. Jim took it personally and acted out by needling the band directly or by hitting the bottle even harder. In a meeting without Morrison, the group decided to hire a bodyguard/drinking buddy/babysitter for Jim, someone who could at least get him to the studio and guard him against his worst demons. The answer seemed to be ex-Dylan roadie Bobby Neuwirth, who was hired under the pretense of filming a piece on the Doors. The three members of the band paid half of Neuwirth's salary, while the record company picked up the rest.

Interestingly, they all assumed that Morrison was too wasted to figure out the ruse. He wasn't but acted the part and waited to see what happened. He continued his onslaught of LA's booze supply and eventually convinced Bobby that his way was much more fun. The two went on an epic binge or what F. Scott Fitzgerald would have called a "spree." Jim's absenteeism got worse. He even brought groupies and sycophants back to the studio, which enraged his bandmates. Manzarek later recalled, "all was well with the creative process . . . except for Jim's drinking."

With Jim too drunk to write or focus the right energy on new lyrics, the band combed his notebooks searching for snippets or poems they could turn into a song. The pressure intensified to get a song out, so they decided to release "The Unknown Soldier" as a single. Elektra even ponied up for a video of the song with Jim's staged execution taking place at the ocean's edge.

Even as fighting in Vietnam escalated, however, many radio stations shied away from the song's overt antiwar message: "Bullet strikes the helmet's head" and the soldier is dead. Even in an era of bedlam, there are dissenters that go too far. Radio stations weren't willing to risk losing the advertising dollars that kept them running. As a result, the song did well—cracking the top forty at thirty-nine—but not becoming the runaway hit Elektra hoped for.

Jim's arrest and subsequent beating in Vegas set an odd tone for the band. The recording sessions exacerbated the schisms that had developed between the three musicians on one side and Jim on the other.

Perhaps the violence, anger, and confusion in the band mirrored the brewing national crisis. For the first time since the Great Depression, many wondered if the nation was becoming undone. Some critics were more pointed: could the United States survive the chaos the year wrought? The stressors that had been building since mid-decade just might bring down the whole country.

We might look back on this era and see the ubiquitous malaise. But that could have also been fear—of getting drafted, of being obliterated in nuclear hellfire, of overdosing on bad acid, of growing up to be one's parents, of getting caught up in the capitalist machine—plus a slew of other nightmares. Today it seems like the time between JFK's murder and 1968 was long, but those years rushed by in an instant for young people in the Sixties. Who could remain optimistic when Kennedy's assassination and the specter of the draft hung over the era like an impermeable haze?

Whatever joy seemed possible—the exploration of self, community, and society—came alive at the intersection of music, drugs, and sex. All three took America's young on a spiritual trip and tamped down the fear, even if just for a moment. The Beatles had touched off that existential overture, Dylan had given it meaning and purpose, the Stones made it apocalyptic, and the Doors turned it into an elemental battle for your soul.

Technological advances allowed music to score each person's quest. A billion dollars of records were sold in 1967, doubling the amount of a decade earlier. Television provided the visual environment, essentially turning the world into a little square window. You could see the heartbreak as the streets of America burned following Martin Luther King Jr.'s assassination in Memphis. A boy dying in the jungles of Vietnam was no farther away than your living room. Technology made the world smaller and more intimate. Newspapers were filled with casualty reports, allowing the community to join in a family's desolation and wonder if their turns were next.

In the middle of all this chaos were the young people, virtually indecipherable to their parents and other authority figures. Yet internally they yearned for meaning in a world that offered little. Hair, clothes, and attitude were symbols that devolved into a kind of signal to those who didn't get it and gave them a reason to forgo actual understanding. Even Robert Kennedy felt the generational divide. As he contemplated his 1968 presidential run, the man who stood beside his brother during the Cuban Missile Crisis received letters flatly stating: "Nobody wants a hippie for President."

Though the Doors struggled to create their third album, Morrison's star remained on the rise. Glowing tributes in newspapers nationwide heralded him as a dark shaman and poet who had his fingers on the pulse of America's youth. The fans didn't see him as a falling-down drunk struggling to remain upright on the walk up La Cienega Boulevard on his way to Room 32 in the Alta Cienega Motel, a hovel and hideaway near the band's offices and rehearsal studio.

In February, *Los Angeles Times* reporter Digby Diehl wrote glowingly of Jim's pale, soft-featured face, encircled with curling long hair and streaked with sweat." He noted: "Teen magazines gush over him with a warmth of unconsciously libidinal praise not seen since Elvis Presley. The *Village Voice* calls him the first major male sex symbol since James Dean died."

But there was no angelic Jim without the demonic, dark Morrison. Diehl described a Doors concert in almost religious terms, explaining, "In a flash, the singer's moment of tranquility dissolves, as if the infernal spirits had once again seized his innocent body." And then, "He explodes with a raw scream, contorting face and torso, rising on his toes as if rigid with stabbing pain, clutching the mic, then doubling over, grasping his groin." Diehl's review was syndicated nationally, so it got wide readership and gave added power to his portrait of Jim as the living embodiment of seduction, charisma, and drug-fueled perception. When another reporter asked him about dressing in black, Jim responded softly, "Well, I used to wear black clothes and that's kind of symbolic of evil. But I think it's the music. It's pretty powerful and it has a certain intensity about it—but I think that it's intense rather than evil or dangerous."

In the spring, after King's murder and the resulting riots, the musical *Hair* opened on Broadway, shocking audiences with both female and male nudity and overt sexuality but also providing older adults a glimpse inside the lives and minds of young people. The Doors gave mainstream America a similar sense of alarm. Bob Rose of the *Chicago Daily News* explained how Jim captured young listeners' attention with a mix of "erotic-filled protest poetry, his charisma and an effective voice."

What Jim and his bandmates captured in 1967 with the first two albums and struggled to replicate in *Waiting* was a delicate balance of retaining (or capturing) the hearts and minds of young people while also remaining aloof to the business-capitalistic elements of the music business. In other words, heavy on the "erotic politicians" talk while staying away from discussion about private jets, gate profits, and cash advances. In late 1968, each member of the band had been handed a fifty-thousand-dollar advance—they were now wealthy young men and bound to get richer.

Journalist Robb Baker outlined their widespread appeal, saying, "Even Dick Clark calls them the biggest group since the Beatles." Around the same time, Morrison stayed on a more ephemeral plane and discussed the visions he sometimes had while on stage: "I looked out in the audience and I had the strangest image. I saw the men all in uniforms and just sitting, and all the girls seemed to me like ultra-flowers. Here's a gray uniform and right beside it the flower of a woman." Whether Jim was messing with a reporter or genuinely had this experience, the mysticism aura spoke to fans because he had spent so much time creating that image. He could talk about the beauty of art and poetry in esoteric ways that might have adults rolling their eyes, but young people wanted to view the world differently, and they believed in his vision.

By the end of May, the Doors had finished *Waiting*, sort of slogging through the process until they had enough material that was album worthy. They also got back on the road, attempting to deliver a magical experience for fans, pushing themselves deeper into the music and testing whatever boundary Jim discovered that evening. For example, in Tucson late in the month, a power failure dropped the baseball stadium into darkness. Later, a single light snapped back on, and Jim started spinning the microphone in wide arcs, almost nailing Manzarek.

Whether he was bored or just seeing where his power might take the night, Jim urged fans to join him onstage. The police in charge of guarding the band demurred. First, they created a phalanx around the stage to prevent the charge of teen bodies. When security was overwhelmed, they retreated to the stage themselves. Jim and his bandmates were surrounded by cops as they closed out the show. This type of crowd manipulation was happening more frequently as Jim goaded audiences to rush the stage. A local journalist emphasized the magical fusion of Morrison's image and antics and the band's tight sets, saying, "The whole situation began to take on an atmosphere of unreality." As for Jim, showmanship mixed with attitude: "Singer-warlock Jim Morrison, wearing skintight leather pants, a peacoat, and a sullen expression, leaped up the side stairs, faked a spastic stumble crossing the stage, and lurched into the lyrics in a slightly hoarse voice. It is undeniably compelling."

Although Jim was never fully comfortable in big venues, the Doors began to play larger arenas. As one of America's top touring acts in an age of live music, they were well paid. At some sold-out gigs the band pulled in thirty-five thousand dollars or more a night (estimated at more than a quarter of a million in today's money).

In June, ahead of the full-album release, the band released "Hello, I Love You" with "Love Street" as the B-side. Unlike "Unknown Soldier," a serious, dark antiwar song with its shocking execution scene, "Hello" was geared toward the pop market. One journalist noted that the new singles were "both happy rock sounds," but that distinction polarized fans. For younger listeners, the upbeat tune was a perfect example of how the Doors brand of psychedelic rock could be turned mainstream. Longtime fans, however, reacted how they have for all eternity—with derision and making claims that the Doors had sold out. This response is typical of critics who believe anything the masses enjoy is beneath them and their ability to detect authenticity.

"Hello, I Love You" rocketed up local, regional, national, and international singles charts. In the band's home base of California, the song jumped onto top-five lists seemingly overnight.

The mixed critical reaction to "Hello" seems jaded looking back more than fifty years later. While the song doesn't carry the gravitas of "Unknown Soldier" or hold the heft of the proto-punk/hard-rock edge of "Five to One," the lyrics are deceptively clever. Just as important, Robby's fuzzy opening riff had a twofold effect of making the song instantly recognizable and hummable. Spinning the radio dial, listeners pinpointed "Hello" as a Doors tune—only the Doors could have made that sound.

The single came to life in the pre-Doors stage of Ray and Jim's partnership when Rick & the Ravens was still an entity. While at the beach, they noticed a beautiful Black woman walking down the street. Ray allegedly asserted she was too young to hit on and Morrison was too shy. Instead of talking to her, Jim wrote his response as if he had the guts to speak up.

An interesting twist lyrically takes the song from a semi-creepy situation of two college grads watching a young girl stroll down the beach to a song of empowerment. As a matter of fact, "she" throughout the tune is the one in power, not the male narrator. She's so beautiful men can't think straight. She's so wonderful the sidewalk itself must bend to watch her go by, just hoping she notices. The hapless narrator, like Morrison and Manzarek that day in the hot sand and sun, is left wondering who she is, this "queen of the angels" who is completely aloof to his longing. He laughs at himself, questioning whether he really thinks he could ever have a chance with her.

Featuring a close-up of Jim's face on the sleeve (one of the iconic "young lion" photos), "Hello" climbed the *Billboard* charts, reaching the top spot on August 3, 1968. It held the position for the next two weeks, eventually selling more than a million copies. "Hello" knocked the instrumental "Grazing in the Grass" by Hugh Masekela from its perch after holding the spot for two weeks.

Looking for new ways to market the band, Jac Holzman at Elektra promoted the single as one of the first to be released in the then nearly unheard of forty-five rpm "stereo" form. Although extremely popular among fans, early forty-fives were recorded in mono and the radio stations were set up to play 45s in that format. As technology evolved, what everyone referred to as a single—would be in stereo and offer a new way of hearing the music. "Hello" was the Doors second single to reach the vaunted position and the first Morrison wrote. Ray later said that he knew the song would be a hit back when Jim wrote it in 1965.

Interestingly, while "Hello" was number one, Jose Feliciano's remake of "Light My Fire" was also in the top five. On several local and regional charts, the strength of the single helped the Doors' first album jump back on the best-selling lists. While critics continued to lambast the single, it also drew criticism for Krieger's alleged theft of the riff from the Kinks song "All Day and All of the Night," a big hit several years earlier. But, despite some controversy, Ray Davies didn't make a big deal out of it, saying that Morrison's apology was enough for him (though the Kinks and Doors attorneys worked out a royalties deal to keep the exposure to a minimum). Ironically, Krieger later said he had a different song in mind, Cream's "Sunshine of Your Love," a hit a year earlier.

"People Got to Be Free" by the Rascals upended "Hello's" run at the top. Upbeat and filled with glitzy horns, the song appealed to yearning for peace, freedom, and tolerance. It stayed on top for five weeks and sold four million copies. Like many Sixties anthems, "People Got to Be Free" had its origins in the dark side of the era. The band had a run-in with a group of country boys when their tour bus stopped for repairs in Fort Pierce, Florida, a seaside community on the Atlantic. Band members were threatened and disparaged for having long hair and beards, a familiar confrontation throughout the decade.

A week before the Doors released *Waiting*, they played a high-profile, sold-out show at LA's Hollywood Bowl on July 5. They had spent weeks rehearsing and put in the extra time to really give the new album a push after plodding through its creation. There would be many stars and celebrities in the eighteen-thousand-person audience. The band upgraded their sound system, adding amplifiers and wattage that would have the Doors sound bouncing across the hills and canyons. Noting the many greats who had played the Hollywood Bowl (but not many rock bands), including the world's greatest orchestras, Ray said getting to perform there "was a great honor."

Before the concert, the whole band went out to a Chinese restaurant with Mick Jagger, a kind of nod from rock royalty that the Doors were a band to be reckoned with. In retrospect, though, crossing paths with Mick was a mistake. He was up to his devilish, competitive best. One rationale for Jagger's actions may have been that he was angry that "Hello, I Love You" had displaced "Jumpin' Jack Flash" on many singles charts. The Doors song was the one fans were humming and the music industry was talking about. Or, maybe Mick just saw Jim as a knockoff of himself and wanted to assert his dominance.

According to Robby, Mick spent most of the evening talking to Jim and flirting with Pam, which pissed off Jim. Of course, Morrison was too cool—or starstruck—to say anything to Jagger. Instead, he did what he routinely did when he fought or argued with Pam—he got loaded. Jim had performed countless times on LSD or drunk, but the acid he took that night seemed to knock the wind out of him. Jim didn't bother to mention taking the acid to the rest of the band, but they figured it out pretty quickly.

In full Lizard King garb—skintight red leather pants, a stunning silver concho belt, and a dark collarless shirt—Jim looked down at the first row. There he spied Mick and Pam cuddling and generally making a scene; some reports even alleged that she was in his lap. Jim probably didn't know it, but this was a typical Jagger move. He liked to assert his dominance by messing around with or outright bedding other guys' partners. It would seem that Jim could hold it together or that the appearance of a Rolling Stone wouldn't mean that much if you're in the Doors—arguably the hotter band at the time—but that wasn't the case. Robby explained: "It's intimidating enough to have Mick Jagger staring up at you while you're trying to perform; you don't need the added worry of him going home with your girl at the end of the night."

The Hollywood Bowl show was a microcosm of the band's future. The musicians had put in their reps and were hyped for a brilliant concert that would clearly make them America's rock-and-roll kings, especially in front of a hometown, star-studded audience. But Jim couldn't handle the pressure or simply underperformed. Some would later charge that Morrison self-sabotaged the concert, which Krieger doubted. "Either way," the guitarist noted, "he mainly stayed glued to his mic stand, rather than jumping all over the place as usual." The concert footage, later released as a documentary along with an album, shows a restrained Morrison, though the band sounds fantastic behind him. A review of the show in the *Los Angeles Times* said Jim "seemed detached and subdued and mildly amused . . . too good-humored to work into the catatonic state which characterizes his most hypnotic—and frightening—performances."

The devilish Jagger got his way too. Later asked what he thought of the Doors, Mick cryptically said, "They were nice chaps, but they played a bit too long." Definitely a backhanded compliment from one of rock and roll's reigning kings. Some media reports and gossip columnists tried to turn the meeting of the two titans into a battle, saying that Mick actually said the concert was "a bore."

John J. Miller, a syndicated columnist, went so far as to say that Mick and Jim "swear they will beat each other bloody the next time they meet," after "Jagger walked out in the middle of the Doors' recent Hollywood Bowl concert, shouting that he was bored by their bad music." The exaggeration may have sold newspapers, but enough witnesses were on-site to contradict the claim.

There are also no reports that Mick and Pam went home together that night either. Certainly, Mick had other calls later that evening, even if the Doors show put him a little behind schedule.

Sunday, July 7, 1968: Despite being banned from the Ed Sullivan Show, the Doors performance from a year earlier is rebroadcast.

Waiting for the Sun was released on July 12, already having had 750,000 preorders sold. Many critics chalked the whole thing up to a band coasting on its reputation. Jim Miller, reviewing the album in *Rolling Stone*, summed up the critical response, saying, "the new record isn't really terrible, it isn't particularly exciting either." Despite these reviews, fans responded and bought *Waiting* in droves.

What critics didn't seem to get was that *Waiting* was decidedly *not* the first two albums. At a pace that would be considered irrational today, the album was the band's third release in eighteen months. It can be argued that "Hello, I Love You" is an all-time Doors classic, "Love Street" captures perfectly the softer side of the Sixties, "Not to Touch the Earth" mirrors the decade's turmoil, and the two antiwar songs—"Five to One" and "The Unknown Soldier"—show the Doors' evolution and willingness to protest society's misdeeds.

Although Jim denied "Five to One" was political, its lyrics prove otherwise and the song could be considered an early form of punk rock, particularly with its call for revolution. Morrison advocates for war between the young and old, which will cause a bloodbath. No matter how many are shot down, the side with the larger numbers ultimately prevails.

In the third stanza Morrison uses a voice that fans have never heard before, a faux British accent that will become popular among American punk bands in the Seventies and Eighties. He laments the fate of the planet in the image of a woman whose best days have passed. She holds a flower of hope but feels misunderstood. Humanity hurtles along, but the aging planet gasps and chokes as darkness stands on the horizon.

Jim also showed his sociopolitical views by admonishing the listener for trading their lives for small change. The only hope to fight against a system that controls the guns and money is to organize. Morrison then conflates the critique of American society with his desire to fulfill his needs through loving his girl. The question at the heart of the song is, should we fight a battle when the war is determined or just focus on our own lives and loves? Vietnam in the Sixties was never out of mind for very long.

Even Bob Dylan was battling to interpret the negativity of 1968, later writing about the chaos he felt at home and around the globe, saying, "If you saw the news, you'd think that the whole nation was on fire." Given his tempestuous relationship with the press, he blamed them for not only "fanning the flames of hysteria" but for anointing him a spokesperson for the age without his consent. "That was funny," he explained, "All I'd ever done was sing songs that were dead straight and expressed powerful new realities. . . . Being true to yourself, that was the thing. I was more a cowpuncher than a Pied Piper."

Morrison was a different Pied Piper for a different audience. The Doors invaded the music scene in parallel with the expansion of the war in Vietnam and its stranglehold on the nation's consciousness. There was no way to unravel the fighting in Southeast Asia and the global protest movement from what was happening in popular culture. Dylan was on one side as a kind of cultural activist, but people knew the Doors understood the chaos and darkness that ensued when war was let loose.

The Doors seemed at the center of the action, equally popular with the troops waging war and the protestors picketing on college campuses and in their communities. Listeners could latch onto whatever feeling or emotion they perceived in the songs. Fire, death, chaos, darkness battled right beside love, tenderness, and care for the environment. Dylan made you think of humanity; Morrison told you your house was on fire.

In 1968 Vietnam was at the heart of America's existential days and nights. January's Tet Offensive, a series of more than a hundred coordinated surprise attacks on cities, towns, and bases in South Vietnam, changed how the public saw the war. The people began to doubt the generals and other military leaders who assured them that the war would soon be won. More important, about half the public turned on President Johnson. The other half wanted escalation to ensure that America emerged victorious.

The year would become *the most* in many respects—as in, most costly ($77 billion), most soldiers killed (16,592), and most troops "in country" (549,500). If one accepts the premise that Vietnam forever changed America (continuing to reverberate through to now), then 1968 is its pivotal year. And though other giants loomed on the music scene in 1968, the Doors loomed larger.

"My beautiful friend, the end . . ."

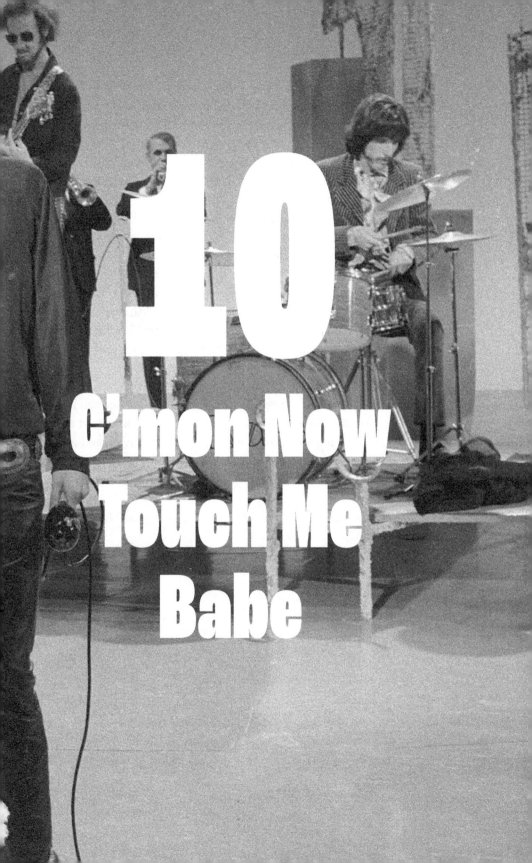

10

C'mon Now
Touch Me
Babe

f 1967 was the Summer of Love, the scene by 1969 had devolved into something darker, more sinister. The ugliness of the year before continued unabated, setting the nation—and the world—on a downward slide. While it seemed as if democracy itself was in peril, the nation attempted to make sense of the debacle in Vietnam and the antiwar battles raging in the streets. The outcome the Doors had predicted in "When the Music's Over" was about to come true—the end, my friend.

Yet the Doors as a rock band should have been riding high, regardless of the existential angst they carried. Their music mattered, and it brought to light many of society's deepest challenges. They had a voice that was different from Dylan or hard-core activist leaders but was influential, nonetheless. They exposed parts of ourselves and our country that we didn't want to confront. Sun, moon, run—just run, 'cause there's no hope!

Fans had responded by making *Waiting for the Sun* the band's first number one album. But, as Robby Krieger recalled, they shouldn't have been surprised at what happened next:

> In a way, it's almost a tragedy that *Waiting for the Sun* ended up being our only album to hit number one. . . . It normalized everything . . . gave Jim an excuse not to change his behavior, and it gave the rest of us an excuse to ignore it. We were happy when we heard we had topped the charts. Maybe we shouldn't have been.

In this unique moment, after all they had accomplished, Jim Morrison was unraveling.

"I am the Lizard King. I can do anything."
—Jim Morrison

The bad mojo of 1968 continued into 1969 for the United States and for the Doors. The band had ended the year spending several months trying to put together *Soft Parade*, their fourth album. As with *Waiting*, they scrambled to write and record amid the chaos of travel and sold-out arenas. The tight unit that had scored unthinkable success was overrun with the vestiges of fame, pressure to outdo earlier efforts, and myriad groupies and hangers-on pulling them apart.

While Ray, Robby, and John seemed to handle success reasonably well, Jim slipped deeper into a world of self-discovery and self-actuation that was driven by alcohol and drugs.

According to Krieger:

> Jim's drinking was at its peak when we were putting together *The Soft Parade*. We were used to alcohol affecting his behavior, but now it was affecting his creative output. He wasn't writing, and he had run out of old material. It meant I had to step up to fill in the song-writing gaps. Which was fine by me. But it threw off the balance that made our other records work so well.

What seemed most at odds with Morrison was how he viewed himself as an erstwhile poet and thinker versus what his life had become as a rock hero and celebrity. He had no family ties and his relationship with Pam, by all accounts, was a constant struggle. He saw himself as a poet, but the world only wanted the Lizard King. John Updike famously claimed that celebrity was a mask that ate into the face, and Jim was dealing with the ramifications of his image outgrowing—and in some ways overtaking—who he felt he was deep down.

Morrison also faced the warring impulses of a gifted thinker attempting to examine his life and future while deadening those efforts with alcohol. According to neuropharmacology professor David Nutt, one of today's leading authorities on the science of alcohol, the drug turns on the system in the brain that makes people feel relaxed, so it reduces social anxiety and self-doubt and removes inhibition and fear. Booze also switches off parts of the frontal cortex responsible for controlling what we do, which leads to greater amounts of consumption, propelling the vicious cycle. Finally, alcohol triggers dopamine—just like cocaine—which is a stimulant leading to exhilaration. All of this, especially the cocaine-like effect that alcohol has, is instructive when thinking about Jim's decision-making at the time (even if it may seem somewhat obvious).

Was Jim a poet, a singer in a pop band, a budding filmmaker, a future actor, a friend, a lover, a star? In the still of the night, how did Morrison see himself and how did he contend with the consequences of that self-image versus what the public saw? His physical transformation mirrored his mental state. He grew a bushy beard and wore layered, earth-tone clothes to hide his weight gain.

The Soft Parade sessions were trying for each band member as well as Paul Rothchild and Bruce Botnick. Each successive record seemed to take more time and energy. The producer compounded the work by demanding take after take in search of perfection, which drove a wedge between him and the band.

The final months of 1968 were consumed with touring and recording. The lingering effects of *Sgt. Pepper's* hung in the studio, so, under Rothchild's guidance, the Doors experimented and then experimented some more. The strain worsened. For Robby, whose guitar was responsible for much of the unique Doors sound, the sessions were monotonous and derivative. "It felt like we were copying the Beatles," he said. "Or worse: copying the Stones when they were copying the Beatles." Jim reacted by staying away altogether.

Rothchild attributed the challenges with the sessions to Jim's apathy. "Jim was really not interested," he said. "When we made *The Soft Parade*, it was like pulling teeth to get Jim into it." While this was true to a degree, the producer's unyielding focus had caused backlash.

The Soft Parade also signaled deeper issues at the heart of the Doors ethos. For the first time, the songwriting credits were listed individually rather than collectively. More disconcerting—as fans and critics would soon learn—the experimentation included adding strings, horns, and saxophones on top of what the band crafted.

Ray remembered that after a lot of problems, including Jim claiming he was "having a nervous breakdown," the trouble started to clear and the whole band was set to take on its biggest tour, which would begin in Miami, in Jim's home state. According to the keyboardist, Morrison "was back to his usual creative, witty, intellectual self." From his perspective, "the Doors were a unit again." But, as Ray would later realize, the brief calm wouldn't last.

If there's one moment in the history of the Doors—and rock music—that has been debated, argued, and analyzed, it is the infamous concert in

Miami on March 1, 1969. If Morrison was already self-destructing, the gig and its fallout fast-tracked him to the end.

The pressure of recording the new album contributed to what ultimately happened in Miami, but there were other factors that have often been overlooked. In the month leading up to the show, Jim got arrested in LA for drunk driving. Then he attended a series of performances at USC by a group called the Living Theater. Founded in 1947, the acting troupe used their show as a way to question societal norms through everyday actions that would overthrow the system. With much audience interaction, they shed clothing, staged dramatic poetry readings, and led anarchistic improvisational interludes. Morrison watched—and participated—with wide eyes. He had found his true north. Their focus on confrontation matched his own. What he saw unfold gave him ideas for enacting his own version of the troupe within the boundaries of a Doors show.

What was becoming clearer to his bandmates and others around him was that there were two factors driving Jim's mood and actions—his rapport with Pam and how much booze he consumed. Each served the other, frequently combining into a combustible mixture of love, hate, agony, and release. Leading up to the Miami show, the couple fought, which cancelled a scheduled vacation they had planned. Jim's response to the turmoil was to get bombed—countless drinks on the plane, more during a layover in New Orleans, more missed flights, and additional drinks. By the time he finally arrived at the Dinner Key Auditorium in Miami, Morrison was blitzed. Promoters had stuffed fifteen thousand people into a decommissioned naval air hanger on a night that eyewitnesses remembered as extremely hot and humid.

Jim took the stage and lashed out at the concertgoers. "He was at once berating the audience for their childlike acceptance of both authority and the status quo," Manzarek remembered. "At the same time imploring them to love one another . . . and him."

With the bewildered crowd ready to stampede, Jim called out: "Love! Love! Love!" but he hurled insults, imploring them to revolt, to riot, to break free of whatever chains entrapped them. When they looked on wide-eyed and dumbfounded, he snapped, "How long are you going to let them rub your face in the shit of the earth?" Nearly apoplectic, he told them they were slaves and enjoyed being beaten down. The crowd surged toward the singer, simultaneously repelled and attracted to him as he spewed invective.

In early 1969, using the word "fuck" and other expletives wasn't common. Eyewitnesses at the show assumed—as Lenny Bruce had in the 1950s—that Morrison would be arrested for his illicit language.

Not quite sure how to react, Ray, Robby, and John attempted to get Jim on track as they had in the past when he was too drunk or stoned. They felt the wooden stage shake. They launched into "Touch Me," mistakenly believing Morrison would sing along. It was too late. He was gone. Madness took over.

As he called out for "dancing in the street," more love, and a summer filled with fun, Jim began tugging at his clothes. Ray, instinctively realizing what was about to happen, called to Vince Treanor to stop Morrison, and the two struggled in unison as the crowd watched. Jim yelled out about exposing himself—"Anybody want to see my cock?"—and the frenzied audience screamed its approval.

If the preceding few minutes could have been called chaotic, the next were a gates-of-hell rage. The singer pretended to expose himself several times, but it was all playacting. Ray, who had the closest view, explained: "That son of a bitch Jim Morrison had teased and taunted and cajoled that crowd into believing he had shown them his cock. Hell, he had hypnotized them. . . . The lying dog Jim Morrison had conned them."

With the sound of "Light My Fire" in the background, Jim didn't stop. Now he wanted a riot and urged the crowd to rush the stage. The police and University of Miami football players guarding the stage were quickly confronted with wild-eyed teens who wanted to get to their hero. "Bodies kept hurtling and charging and flailing about," Ray said. Jim was thrown from the stage and danced with the crowd like a shaman. The house lights came up and Manzarek stopped playing. John had already left the stage, and Robby wrapped his arms around his guitar as a way to protect it from the onrush.

Jim had lit the night on fire. You might suspect that Miami was a deliberate attempt by a very smart, very drunk man to sabotage or excise the part of himself he could no longer stand. He later told *Circus* magazine, "I think I was just fed up with the image that had been created around me." Although he cooperated with its creation and—it can be argued—orchestrated its design, he complained, "It just got too much for me to really stomach. . . . I just put an end to it in one glorious evening." This retrospection, though, happened after he'd sat through a lengthy trial and had a year and a half to think about why he did it.

While the events leading up to Miami put him on a downward trajectory, it is hard to imagine that Jim realized he'd just lit the fuse that would ultimately destroy him.

~~🦎~~

Larry Mahoney, a *Miami Herald* journalist, reviewed the show on March 3, reporting that Jim had not incited a riot and afterward, backstage, "nobody tried to arrest Morrison." He interviewed Charles Crocker, a Miami police officer, who said nothing of the alleged indecent exposure and instead remarked, "That guy did his damnedest to start a riot and the kids didn't move." Mahoney did claim, however, that "Morrison appeared to masturbate in full view of his audience, screamed obscenities, and exposed himself." Yet none of the thirty-one police officers moved to arrest the singer.

Three days later, on March 6, Mahoney reported that six warrants had been issued, including one for a felony—lewd and lascivious behavior in public by exposing his genitals and by simulating masturbation and oral copulation." If given the maximum sentence for the charges, Morrison would serve three and a half years in jail. State Attorney Richard E. Gerstein announced that Florida would pursue "the maximum sentence on each count to run consecutively."

The public outcry was huge. For the Doors, the national tour that would finally deliver them to the masses in style—and bring in huge box-office receipts—was cancelled when venue owners and operators caved to the pressure from local politicians, parents' groups, and decency activists. In effect, they were banned. Or as one rock historian explained: "The Doors were show business poison."

On April 3, Morrison turned himself into the FBI at its LA office. He was released after posting a five-thousand-dollar bond. With Jim's freedom at stake, the media took a curious stance: They reported on the reaction against him but also painted the rock star alternately as a caricature of the gluttonous, idiot celebrity and the scourge of 1960s America. As the negativity spread, radio stations pulled Doors songs from the air and parents' groups spurred teens to hold "burn the Doors" album events to show their disgust.

While the Doors became public enemy number one after Morrison's arrest, it must be remembered that at the same time, nearly twelve thousand American military personnel had been killed in Vietnam. From a contemporary vantage point, the Miami incident seems like an overt case of pinning an era on an incident that really didn't have very large stakes. For example, in the months after Miami, sex, drugs, and nudity were given a starring role in the film *Midnight Cowboy*. Later in 1969, *Easy Rider* contained many counterculture ideas, including the use of psychedelics. In light of Morrison's arrest and the ban on the Doors, it seemed to be that America had divided itself into two factions: pro- and anti-hippie. The two couldn't be reconciled. Conservative forces in Miami realized they could use the fact that there were young teens in the Dinner Key Auditorium audience to strike out against the counterculture by delivering justice against the Lizard King.

After Miami, neither Jim nor his bandmates would ever be the same again. The fissures in their relationship and in Jim's booze-fueled explorations of his own psyche were brought to the surface. The specter of jail time became ever-present, which choked the air from Morrison's life and upended his relationships.

Robby said, "Jim's drinking had ramped up gradually since the beginning of the band, but in the wake of the Miami incident it was isolating him from the rest of us and making it hard to be his bandmate, let alone his friend." Although they had a difficult time expressing it to Jim in that moment, given that his actions got them banned and had cut off their income, the three bandmates were sympathetic. "We felt bad for him. We weren't happy about being pulled off the radio or having our shows cancelled, but after the initial wave of bad press, the whole thing actually made us look cool, and it was easy enough to bounce back," the guitarist explained. There was life after Miami—as long as Jim didn't end up in jail.

Still, a band is a business—kind of like a mini-corporation—and there were many bills to pay and people to support. *The Soft Parade* reportedly cost about eighty-six thousand dollars to produce (about seven hundred thousand dollars today). After the fact, the series of cancelled gigs later cost the band at least a million dollars and possibly much more. The Doors organization also faced lawsuits as promoters attempted to recoup the money they had spent publicizing upcoming shows. Fighting those legal battles cost the band in attorney fees, in addition to the fees for Jim's impending defense.

Attorney Robert Josefsberg, who would serve as co-counsel in Jim's defense, offered a different perspective, "I'm angry at the Doors management team for letting him go onstage. He was drunk and they shouldn't have let him out there." They could have kept Morrison from performing, but, as the lawyer contended, "they wanted to make the money." From this perspective, the need to keep the Doors machine running almost destroyed everything they had created. And it ultimately played a role in Jim's death.

Released in July after all the fanfare and negative publicity, *The Soft Parade* was as polarizing for Doors fans as Jim's arrest had been for the general public. This was not the American *Sgt. Pepper's*—or even a good knockoff. Critics were brutal, unable to comprehend how the band of the sublime debut album could create this one.

Although it didn't have a big hit single beyond "Touch Me," which had reached number three on *Billboard* and number one on *Cash Box* prior to the Miami incident, *The Soft Parade* still reached number six on the album charts and went gold, the Doors fourth straight record to achieve that distinction. The new record also helped the band to gradually win back concert promoters—although with clauses in contracts that fined them for bad behavior. They launched a smaller tour and had a renewed sense of mission after what they had experienced.

The band's vitality on the short tour led observers to wonder what was next for the band, particularly with Morrison's fate undecided.

11

A Real Good Time

The three-day Seattle Pop Festival was held in Gold Creek Park in late July 1969. Crowds streamed into the park, eventually swelling to forty to fifty thousand, though some put the number at a hundred thousand. One journalist claimed it was the biggest rock audience ever gathered in the Pacific Northwest. A pass for the entire festival cost fifteen dollars (about one hundred twenty dollars today). Twenty-five groups were scheduled to appear, ranging from Chuck Berry and Bo Diddley to Vanilla Fudge and the Byrds. The event would eventually gross over three hundred thousand dollars (almost three million dollars today).

Writer Ted Natt wrote at length about the crowd at Gold Creek, which he viewed as a sea of "long hair, dirty clothes, and bare feet." At night, he explained, "Thick clouds of marijuana smoke drifted up from the crowd . . . some were speeding on amphetamines. Others were ripped on LSD."

Vendors lined the outer perimeter of the festival selling everything from jewelry and incense to goat-milk yogurt and hot dogs. Young men selling LSD roamed the crowd, offering a hit for two bucks. An onsite clinic was inundated with people suffering from too much booze or drugs, as well as lesser ailments, primarily heat exhaustion. Six hundred were treated for minor injuries or sunburn during the festival's final two days.

In a strange twist suited for true-crime aficionados, a month after the show, newspapers reported that a murder victim had been found near the festival grounds. The *Tacoma News Tribune* noted the naked young man "had been shot several times in the head." His body was found partially buried about eight hundred yards from the festival site.

Amid the smell of hot dogs and weed, crowds called out for the festival headliner—the Doors. In fact, as the band's set was about to start, the crowd chanted "We Want Morrison!" According to an eyewitness, concertgoers overturned garbage cans and then used them as drums to beat in unison. They screamed themselves hoarse for the singer and band. In the Pacific Northwest, fans were willing to forgive Jim for Miami.

As the crowed swelled in the hope that the Doors would soon appear, members of the press got nervous and searched for escape routes to use in case fans rushed the stage. A thin barrier of chicken-wire fencing lined the area. There was no way it would have held back the rushing crowd, nor would the handful of Black Panthers who were hired to protect the stage.

While fans were eager to see the Doors, journalists at the show were less thrilled, seemingly more interested in not getting trampled than in watching the band. Jim faced a new level of scrutiny following Miami. He sold newspapers and magazines regardless of how he was covered. A smart-aleck contingent of music journalists had an answer for the Doors, particularly coming off the roundly panned *Soft Parade*.

For example, Edd Jeffords claimed:

Once one of the vital influences in rock, the Doors apparently have been captured entirely by the ego-tripping of Morrison . . . the Doors now come on like some kind of carnival sideshow, with Morrison as the geek out front.

When the band initially took the stage, "the geek out front" was nearly unrecognizable for those expecting the Lizard King. Morrison wore a beat-up denim jacket and a scruffy beard. While Ray and John prepped, hitting notes and tapping out quick rhythms, Jim walked across the stage with little fanfare. In fact, he was ignored. According to Jeffords, Morrison looked "old and a little wild." While he waited for the first notes of "When the Music's Over" to start the show, someone claimed that Jim stroked his beard and "smiled evilly" at the young girls in the front row. At that moment, he looked more like Charles Manson—who would gain infamy for leading the gruesome murders in LA about two weeks later—than the Lizard King.

Jeffords noted that Jim's "ego trip" grew as the show progressed—puffing on a cigar and "abusing, insulting, and ridiculing his audience." He kept up a running chatter, calling one heckler a "big-mouthed bastard." The band closed out the set with "The End," but Morrison lingered after the others left the stage. He stood in the spotlight mimicking "Christ on the cross." Journalist Michael Quigley added that the show "wasn't very effective" because of "Morrison's uninvolved performance."

After watching Morrison and his bandmates walk from the stage to a waiting helicopter to chopper them away from the grounds, Jeffords quoted festival organizer Boyd Grafmyre, who stood stunned at Morrison's actions: "That's a quick way for him to make thirty grand." Jeffords was less kind in summing up the spectacle, saying that all the singer had to do was "show his ass on stage in an uptight town, get arrested and become a cult hero to millions of teenyboppers who don't seem to mind being insulted and laughed at."

While the Seattle Pop Festival may have not been a top Doors performance, animus increased as people felt betrayed by Morrison because of Miami or because they believed *The Soft Parade* didn't measure up to previous Doors records. The reaction represented the fickle pop-culture reaction then and now—tear down and criticize an artist for becoming too popular, particularly if they've come from the underground.

Others complained that the 1969 version of Jim Morrison didn't look like the glammed-up rock star in pinups and posters. According to rock historian Bob Spitz, one of those disappointed fans was Led Zeppelin's lead singer Robert Plant, whose band was on the festival undercard. The media had noted similarities between the two singers, and Plant wanted to see Morrison for himself. "Imagine his disillusionment when a bloated Jim Morrison ambled onstage in a skintight black leather jumpsuit and screamed, 'Fuck you all!' at the audience," Spitz wrote.

Plant later recalled:

He hung on the side of the stage and nearly toppled into the audience and did all those things that I suppose were originally sexual things, but as he got fatter and dirtier and more screwed up, they became more bizarre. So it was really sickening to watch. My wife and I were there watching and we couldn't believe it.

The Led Zeppelin singer, like many others, couldn't understand where the Doors and Morrison were headed. In fact, Jeffords called out Ray publicly and in essence said he should dissolve the Doors.

Yet behind the scenes, the chaos in Miami had repercussions that affected everything they did. For example, in Seattle (and every other venue), promoters looked for reasons to not pay the Doors based on Jim's behavior. What's more, local police departments itched to make Morrison an example. In some cities, politicians invoked arcane regulations to stop them from performing. At every turn it was whispered that undercover officers were tracking the band and that the FBI was watching them closely. They couldn't trust the limo drivers, promoters, and anyone else outside their tight circle because they might be narcs—in an era where the law infiltrated every counterculture movement or organization.

Plant and other rock stars—let alone fans—couldn't have imagined the gravity. Ray, Robby, John, and Jim faced legal peril and the band was being used as a political and cultural football by the conservative American establishment. In late 1969, for example, in Vegas—America's sin city of all places, mobbed up and as dirty as any city in the country—a Doors show was almost cancelled by Sheriff Robert Lamb because of Miami. Forty extra security guards were hired to watch the band. Most telling, however, was Lamb's preshow appearance, according to Jerry Hopkins and Danny Sugerman in *No One Here Gets Out Alive*: "with blank warrants made out for each of the Doors, the charges to be filled in—or not—according to how the band performed.

As the summer of 1969 rolled into the fall, the Doors faced the specter of Jim's fate and the challenge of how to move past *The Soft Parade* with a new album. Morrison's instinct was to pull back from the band and search for a new creative outlet. Not surprising, given his degree at UCLA and interest in filmmaking, he found the answer in Hollywood.

Jim had struck up a friendship with poet-novelist Michael McClure, a writer he admired deeply. In fact, it was McClure who had read some of Morrison's work and urged him to publish it, a boost that validated the singer's self-identity. Hoping to get Morrison working as an actor and writer, film insider Bill Belasco hired the two to adapt a screenplay from McClure's unpublished novel, *The Adept*.

Belasco was then a top lieutenant for Jim Aubrey, a former television programming executive who had taken over the top spot at MGM in late 1969. His tenure at CBS had revolutionized the company, taking it to the top of TV ratings on the back of shows he produced, including *The Beverly Hillbillies* and *Gilligan's Island*.

The Aubrey playbook, he explained to *Life* magazine, was centered on the idea that people loved shows based on characters they could identify with:

Feed the public little more than rural comedies, fast-moving detective dramas, and later, sexy dolls. No old people; the emphasis was on youth. No domestic servants, the mass audience wouldn't identify with maids. No serious problems to cope with. Every script had to be full of action. No physical infirmities.

Despite his success at CBS, Aubrey was eventually booted after a series of incidents were uncovered, including unresolved tax issues to accusations about his excessive spending while heading the network. Aubrey's ouster was completed after shareholders learned that he had bought Jackie Gleason an expensive, ultramodern home in Westchester County, fifty miles from the Big Apple.

Although Aubrey was a workaholic with a quick temper and was never fully satisfied with a script, set design, or director, he liked Morrison and told his underlings and others that Jim could become the 1970s version of James Dean. After CBS, Aubrey launched his own production company, then later took over at MGM.

With Aubrey's blessing, Belasco set McClure and Morrison up in a space at 9000 Sunset Boulevard, a twelve-story complex on the border of West Hollywood and Beverly Hills. The high-rise was home to the city's most influential music companies and public relations firms. Out of its floor-to-ceiling windows visitors could see both the downtown skyscrapers of LA and the steep mountains that framed the city.

The gig drew Jim further away from the other members of the Doors and gave him something different to pursue. According to Belasco, there was open discord that bordered on hostility. "The conflict grew out of the Miami incident, for which they all held Jim responsible, and they'd begun to do numbers in their own heads that he had ruined their careers," he remembered. "He was carrying the whole burden on his back . . . they were making it uncomfortable for him." Belasco also claimed that the other Doors knew they owed Jim "because they wouldn't have careers if it hadn't been for Jim Morrison." After Miami, they viewed the singer differently, even though they needed him to keep the band viable.

Many people, including Aubrey, urged Jim to leave the Doors and strike out on his own—as an actor, poet, director, or solo artist—but despite a potential payday of millions of dollars, Morrison stuck with the band. Given the real possibility of jail time, he may have felt that leaving the band would lead to ruin. Given that he had basically cut ties with his parents, maybe Jim needed the now-dysfunctional family that Ray, Robby, and John gave him, despite the distance that had grown between them.

The Doors returned to the studio in the fall of 1969 to record their fifth album. With so many gigs cancelled, Elektra execs wanted to keep the band in the spotlight and hoped they would have a new record out before the holidays. Although they wouldn't meet that deadline, getting back into the studio sparked some of the magical collaboration that had made the Doors so good. According to Ray, "The enforced layoff caused by Miami resulted in a burst of creativity by Jim and Robby. . . . We were having fun again."

Each band member realized that the sessions were key to what they would be in the future. Robby told a story about how the band reassessed themselves as the *Soft Parade* sessions wound down. They had gathered at a nearby Mexican restaurant to refuel. On the strength of margaritas and beer, they went back to the studio and just jammed—like they had in the early days. Playing covers of tunes they loved, the creative spark ignited, and they saw themselves differently—the yoke of the last album was gone. The Doors weren't the Beatles; they didn't need to experiment to make great music. Instead, Krieger noted that the band had to stop what they had been doing and "get back to making music the old-fashioned way."

Ray emphasized the collaboration that had made the early albums so good, particularly Robby's ear for riffs and Jim's lyrics and melody. The foursome seemed back and ready to reignite. When it was time to record, Krieger remembered, "We just got in the studio and jammed, and the songs came together organically." Too many groups had attempted to imitate the Beatles after the success of *Sgt. Pepper's*, but no one could re-create that sound. A backlash was inevitable—a wave of music that stripped away the horns, strings, and multiple tracks in favor of a raw, authentic sound.

Through this notion of authenticity, Ray's influence over the sound permeated the sessions. "I think his Chicago roots informed the music, Chicago blues in particular," explains jazz pianist Evan Palazzo. "Manzarek's basslines are not difficult in terms of execution, but that playing is brilliant in its simplicity. His ability to walk a bassline with the keyboard is extraordinary."

A serious challenge, however, was that Jim's drinking had gotten even further out of control. Reportedly he was hanging around the Whisky each night, drinking until he passed out, and frequently waking up—literally—in a gutter or somewhere on the street. Jim's escapades grew legendary but were also awful and petty. He did horrible things while drunk, such as prodding people into fights or aggressively pouring beer on female fans or urinating in the streets. Siddons recalled a day in the studio that Morrison drank a case and a half of beer without much consequence, similar to how F. Scott Fitzgerald approached drinking beer in the 1930s, dozens at a time—which he believed was a lesser evil than downing fifth after fifth of gin. Jim was in free fall, and no one in the organization had figured out how to help him.

Looking back with a twenty-first-century lens, it's stunning how the people closest to Jim didn't intervene. Even Elektra President Jac Holzman—an adult in a world of twentysomethings and acolytes—said, "Jim was now in another world. He had separated from the rest of us because he had to." A rather cryptic message that lacks urgency in the face of what was clearly an emergency.

It is as if Holzman and the others simply believed they could continue exploiting the cash cow without doing something to help Morrison as a friend and a human being. By all accounts the collective idea was to have him back in the studio to get things back on track.

Sometimes the greats can rise to inhuman levels of accomplishment despite significant obstacles. The sessions that led to *Morrison Hotel* typify that.

"Pure Doors," Ray said. "Pure rock and blues and jazz and soul and love. . . . Hard and fast."

In late November, while the band was putting *The Soft Parade* behind them, the Rolling Stones released *Let It Bleed*. The bluesy, guitar-heavy sound punctuated an American tour that found Mick, Keith, and the band exploring sounds they heard in the United States, including bits of country and gospel.

An exploration of the chaos they felt living part-time in America and elsewhere in the midst of Vietnam, the album contains dark scenes and swirling sounds that reflected the violence and disturbing images people saw on nightly newscasts.

At nearly seven minutes long, "Midnight Rambler" could have been a Morrison song, the evil tale of the Boston Strangler who carries a knife and a gun like a "brainbell jangler" and attacks wantonly without warning. A shocking aspect of the song—labeled "nihilistic gospel" by historian Roger Kimball—is that victims have no hope of escape. The Strangler in Mick's eyes—and accentuated by his wicked harmonica and Richards's chords—may leave footprints behind as he gets closer, but he is also superhuman, able to pound down steel doors to get his prey. As if that weren't enough, Jagger ups the terror by switching perspectives: the question of whether "you" have heard the tale suddenly becomes "me" and "I'll" (as in "I'll stick my knife" into "your" throat).

Although "Midnight Rambler" conjures Morrison, the song isn't an imitation of the Doors. Instead, it reveals that Jim and Mick were drawing from the same source—taking in the dramatic cultural shift that was occurring and reflecting it back at their audiences. Later the Stones found their groove on *Beggars Banquet* (released in December 1968), which was powered by the twin epics of "Sympathy for the Devil" and "Street Fighting Man" and which demonstrated the band's power in creating operatic rock that interpreted the immediacy of the era.

Compared to *The Soft Parade*, with its experimental elements, *Let It Bleed* seems gritty and in the moment. And that said, it's easy to conclude that the power of that record—in addition to that of *Beggars Banquet*—pushed the Doors back to the raw sound of *Morrison Hotel*.

Although they spoke about one other rarely—and though the press attempted to drum up a rivalry between them—it's clear that Jim and Mick were watching each other.

"Our music has returned to the earlier form, using just four instruments. . . . [We] wanted to get back to the original, basic format."
—Jim Morrison

The songs on *Morrison Hotel* have grown in stature over the decades, but that shouldn't overshadow the significance they had in late 1969 and early 1970 when the album was released. Many people—from rock critics to fans who had stood by the group—thought the Doors were done.

They believed that *The Soft Parade* signaled a fall from rock superstardom and an end to the band being compared to the Beatles and Rolling Stones. Then Jim's arrest yanked them off the stage and out of the (fickle) public eye.

There were plenty of bands that hoped to fill the vacuum, from Led Zeppelin and the Allman Brothers to solo artists Neil Young and Rod Stewart. This is the vortex the Doors faced when they recorded and released *Morrison Hotel*.

After *The Soft Parade*, the band reversed course, and the response was immediate. Journalist Michael Cuscuna raved, "It is not the old Doors, nor is it the current commercial Doors; it is Jim Morrison singing some excellent songs, covering territory that the group had not heretofore explored." The focus that Ray emphasized—"pure Doors"—not only restored the band's reputation, it reasserted its place among the world's greats.

A rock-and-blues vibe kicked off on the record's title song, a song Jim wrote from episodes in his own life—from wild driving along LA's twisted canyon roads to his desire for an early morning beer to kickstart the day. "Roadhouse Blues" also showed a new energy in Jim and Robby's creative partnership. "I was fooling around with a riff," the guitarist remembered, "and Jim asked me to play it again while he threw some words over it." There was also a depth to the lyrics that fit the Doors' dark aura, particularly when probing an uncertain future, where "the end is always near."

Adding to the driving beat, they pulled in the legendary guitarist Lonnie Mack—who was either working as a janitor at Elektra and selling Bibles door-to-door or in the Elektra A&R department—to play the bass on "Roadhouse Blues." When the tune hits fifth gear and launches into Robby's guitar solo, Jim spontaneously blurted out "Do it, Robby, do it!" which they kept on the record. The phrase—a favorite of listeners to this day—spawned a bit of controversy. Lonnie Mack, according to Krieger, told everyone who would listen that it was his name Morrison blurted. (Listen for yourself to make your own determination.)

What surprised critics and fans was the range of songs and sounds on *Morrison Hotel*. The album had a gritty, unbridled vibe that fit with the photo of the band on the cover in the window of a cheap flophouse. Although it produced no hit singles to match their past efforts, the album rocked with "You Make Me Real" and the underrated "Ship of Fools" and "Maggie M'Gill."

The original "ship of fools" was a metaphor that Plato used in the *Republic* to interrogate mob mentality and the chaos the masses instigate when they aren't prepared to lead. Katharine Anne Porter used it as the title of a best-selling novel, published in 1962 and made into a 1965 film starring Vivian Leigh and José Ferrer. The well-read Morrison, who watched a lot of films too, may have read or seen *Ship of Fools* and turned it into a song.

In Morrison's hands, the song is a lament for the dying human race but delivered in an upbeat, bouncy tempo that belies its intent. He contrasts the advances people had made getting to the moon with the downfall caused by mishandling the ship of fools. Interestingly, Jim implies that people are completely oblivious to what is happening, worried about the smog, while the ship holds on for dear life. Yet at the same time, what choice do people have to stop the inevitable? Pretty heady stuff for a short bluesy rock song, but "Ship of Fools" demonstrates how Jim's poetry could provoke thought in careful listeners.

Scouring Jim's old notebooks, where he kept his poems and personal narratives, the band put together "Peace Frog," a guitar-forward rocker that could be interpreted as an antiwar anthem, but also a song that supported a woman's right to abortion. Drawing from the recent past, Morrison added lines about blood and New Haven, the terror of the police assaults on the crowds protesting at the 1968 Democratic National Convention, and told the now-mythic story of seeing a truckload of dead Native Americans on the side of the road on a family trip to Albuquerque.

Despite the state of mind Jim was in—because of legal pressures and excessive drinking—what struck people when they heard *Morrison Hotel* was his voice. Hopkins and Sugerman wrote that "Jim was usually drunk during the sessions and it often took all night to record the vocals for one song." Across the album, whether it's the rockers or the ballads, like "Blue Sunday" and "Indian Summer," Morrison used his voice like an instrument, regardless of the effort it took to get the best take on tape. In his vocals there is a mellow but growling edge, a complexity akin to a great bourbon.

When *Morrison Hotel* went gold—the Doors' fifth in a row—no one doubted that the band was relevant again. And the lack of singles on the record helped them reclaim lost ground with music journalists, who equated that with artistic integrity. Soon *Morrison Hotel* would define the Doors' sound.

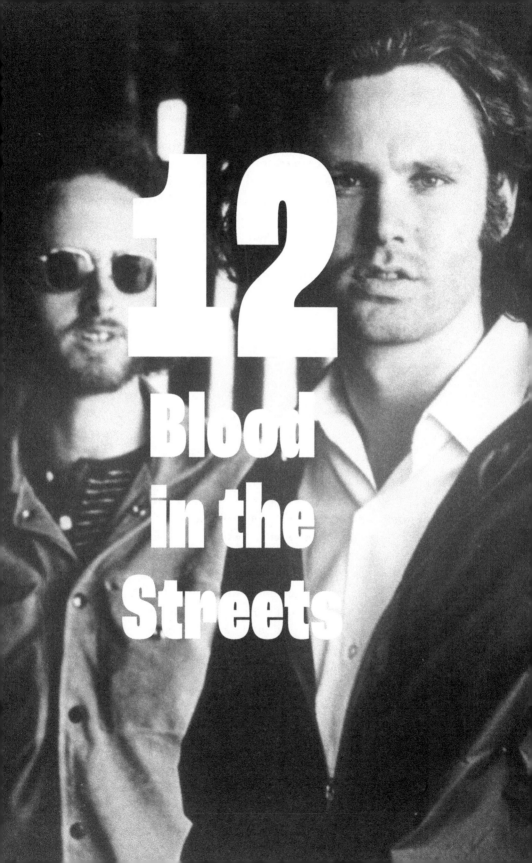

12
Blood in the Streets

When Jim sang about blood in the streets that flowed up to his thighs, listeners may have been shocked at the image—but violence had become common in 1969 and 1970. A long, bloody decade was ending, and what people had considered a chance to create a new society was being erased.

The new decade began, but the Seventies didn't herald better times. Rather, the violence became more wanton and opposing forces became more entrenched—the counterculture versus the establishment. The murders on the campuses of Kent State and Jackson State in early 1970 showed firsthand how the state could meet nonviolent protest with deadly force.

"There is conflict. That's why we have a war and flower children in the same reality. We're part of the war and part of the love-in because it is happening."

—Jim Morrison

Everything that happened in the Sixties—culturally, politically, economically, or socially—must be viewed through the lens of Vietnam. The war and the activism it sparked served as the wellspring for everything that happened thereafter. In 1975, Jonathan Schell attempted to assess the era in the *New Yorker*, explaining: "Wherever the shadow of the war had fallen—and it had fallen nearly everywhere—unity of purpose had been lost and hope had died." In many respects, Vietnam has subsequently haunted the nation, tainted how people think and feel about and understand America, and sunk hope in a sea of fear, anxiety, and violent images.

For Robby, looking back on those dark days, he found solace in how the Doors' music gave soldiers hope, saying, "We've been told repeatedly that our music helped a lot of guys through the absolute worst moments of their lives." The band gave them hope when their government couldn't give them a reason for *why* they were there. As Schell explained, "Although the war was unquestionably at the root of the nation's political disorders, what was at the root of the war itself was obscure . . . the war was as much a symptom of the disorders as it was a cause."

In 1969 those moments Krieger mentioned were particularly harrowing. Bad news from Southeast Asia was constant. While Richard Nixon's war plan to reduce the number of troops brought thousands home, nearly half a million military personnel remained in-country. In total, some forty thousand US citizens had been killed in the war.

The previous fall, on the night he'd been elected, Nixon gloated that he planned to "bring the American people together . . . bridge the generation gap . . . the gap between the races . . . bring America together." But, as with Lyndon Johnson, the Vietnam War handcuffed him to an unwinnable quagmire. Just three weeks before Kent State, Nixon's Republican National Committee published a statement proclaiming that he "has made a dramatic impact on the national spirit . . . visibly altered America's mood and has changed the direction of Government for generations to come." After he had fooled the nation into electing him, saying he would end the war and usher in a peaceful era, Nixon revealed who he truly was when he decided to bomb Cambodia.

What Vietnam wrought on American streets and in cities across the nation was nearly unthinkable. But would protest lead to revolution? As the Doors emphasized in "Five to One," it seemed like the numbers would win, despite the guns being in the hands of the establishment. What Dylan had been doing, what the Doors were doing, and what many other bands and performers had done was to speak truth to power. Around since ancient Greece (called *parrhesia*, "to speak everything") and used by nonviolent actors across history (most notably Gandhi and Martin Luther King Jr.), the concept had been part of many activist movements in US history. But in the late Sixties, the establishment's forces didn't care about the rights of protesters, activists, and others to speak out against injustice.

Instead of debating thoughtfully, the nation descended into rage and violence. Its citizens were more influenced by what they *saw* or *perceived* than what they *experienced*. Countless people, for example, watched the news or read newspapers and felt threatened by hippies, who were typically portrayed as drugged-out, potentially violent anarchists who wanted to take from middle-class America what it valued most. In this environment, a hint of peril soon transformed into an actual threat. During these threatening moments, the state response was often more violent than the incident warranted.

In other words, popular culture and tools of mass communication were driving and shaping the national consciousness—backed by the power and authority of those with the guns. We saw this on full display at Kent State when a relatively minor threat led to an overwhelming—and ultimately murder. The insecurity people felt was intensified by the war in Vietnam and the lies spread by government officials. Americans grew suspicious when they saw death notices in their local newspapers or knew someone who had died in the war, a reality that ran counter to what Lyndon Johnson, Richard Nixon, and others reported.

America had been building toward the Sixties since the end of World War II. A series of events created a tinderbox of anxiety: Hiroshima, the Cold War, the Civil Rights Movement, the Cuban Missile Crisis, and the assassinations that began with the killing of John Kennedy. Collectively, these events shook the faith people had in the system. Historian Joel Rhodes later explained: "The common working-class American just didn't understand. . . . What's happening to the values and traditions we hold dear?"

Given that his father was a career Navy man and eventually a Vice Admiral, Jim Morrison's experience would have been more intense than most people his age. But he also grew up under the specter of nuclear annihilation, was seventeen when JFK took office, in college when he was killed, twenty-two when the first American combat troops were sent to Vietnam, and later drafted. Summing up the emotional consequences on young people, historian Max Elbaum explained: "Those of us who came of age in the '60s lived with pain, fear, and often desperation."

On the cultural front, the events of the Sixties were also threatening because of the sexual revolution, brought on by the introduction of birth control pills, and women's activism, which led to them leaving the home for the workplace. The most violent reaction, however, was against civil rights. The race-related fear induced in the 1950s intensified in the next decade. Regardless of how riots were triggered in urban centers, for example, the media portrayed them from an anti-Black perspective. The not-so-hidden message was that suburbanites should fear these events and protect themselves from *the other* moving into their neighborhoods.

At the end of 1969, two incidents created near-hysteria. It started with the murder rampage in LA launched by cult leader Charles Manson and was followed by the murder of Meredith Hunter, a Black man attending a Rolling Stones outdoor concert in Altamont, California, by members of the Hell's Angels motorcycle gang. (Three others died at the festival, but accidentally.)

Both of these events have been called the "death of the Sixties" by many who believed both tragedies killed the spirit the hippies hoped to instill in a new America, powered by the immense Baby Boomer generation. However brutal these incidents were, though, the next decade had just started when another transformative event took place.

For thirteen seconds on May 4, 1970, Ohio National Guardsmen opened fire on students protesting the Vietnam War at Kent State University in Kent, Ohio, killing four and wounding nine others. What had started as a small campus demonstration—one of thousands nationwide—instantly became a global symbol of the Vietnam era.

The agony of the murders was captured in a Pulitzer Prize–winning photograph—taken just minutes after the shooting by photojournalism student John Filo—in which an anguished young woman knelt over the body of a dead student with her arms raised in despair. For many, this image ended the Woodstock era. Any lingering idyllic notions of the 1960s vanished with Kent State.

The incident began with protest. On April 30, 1970, President Nixon appeared on national television to announce that American troops were invading Cambodia to strike suspected guerrilla strongholds. The new policy contradicted his previous plan, which pledged a "Vietnamization" of the war to gradually reduce America's direct involvement.

Reaction to the escalation was immediate and intense, especially on the nation's college campuses. More than one and a half million students protested the announcement. Rather than address the outrage at the heart of the movement, Nixon called the activists "bums" who were "blowing up the campuses." With this move the president aimed to rally his middle-class supporters against the counterculture.

After the shootings, officials shut down Kent State, which remained closed for the rest of the school year. As news about the tragedy spread, campus unrest escalated nationwide, and about five hundred colleges were eventually closed or disrupted.

Less than two weeks later, another campus shooting occurred at Jackson State University in Mississippi. Again, a relatively minor student protest escalated quickly and ended when police and state officers fired into a dormitory at the all-Black school, killing two students and wounding nine others. The lack of attention given to the massacre at Jackson State embittered many in the Black community.

In June, Nixon formed the President's Commission on Campus Unrest as a way to investigate the shootings on the two campuses. No arrests were made as a result of the probe, however.

Although off to a deadly start, the Seventies weren't like the decade before. In fact, conservative and middle-class Americans retrenched against the counterculture and its principles. Nixon, in particular, skillfully manipulated his supporters and welcomed to his side anyone who had grown tired of the elite, progressive members of the protest movement. He equated Middle America with *us* and the hippies as *them*, then created barriers between the two to ensure that he retained power.

As tension grew between the protesters and establishment, student demonstrators used more-aggressive tactics, which included occupying college offices and buildings. In many cases, the clashes with local police forces resulted in violence, with officers clubbing and roughing up the activists. Jonathan Schell explained that when Nixon convinced mainstream Americans that he would end the war, they turned on protesters. "Convinced that one symptom—the war—was about to disappear, they were all the more eager to have this second symptom disappear too."

Again, Nixon fueled the agitation. At a speech in South Dakota, he railed that America's foundational principles were "under bitter and even violent attack" by agitators. "Drugs, crime, campus revolts, racial discord, draft resistance, on every hand we find old standards violated, old values discarded." Nixon didn't mention how his administration had sowed conflict by not ending the war as he promised. He also left out how he validated the violent crackdown on the counterculture. At other presidential addresses in mid-1970, Nixon threatened military engagement to "strike back" against agitators.

With all the chaos in the country and Jim still facing an uncertain future, the Doors decided to record a live album at shows between July 1969 and May 1970. The record was released on July 20, 1970, and was ironically titled *Absolutely Live*—because the album consisted of many shows edited together by Paul Rothchild (though the listener would not have known otherwise). Jim liked the effort, calling it "a fairly true document of what the band sounds like on a fairly good night . . . an above-average evening." *Absolutely Live* eventually climbed to number eight on the *Billboard* album list in September.

The Doors began the project in mid-1969 at two sold-out shows at the Aquarius Theater in Los Angeles. Throughout the performance Morrison was a more sedate version of himself. Gone was the jumping and shaman-like dancing of earlier years. Instead, he sat on a stool, smoked a cigar, and belted out song after song with newfound intensity.

Listening to those first recordings, the Doors determined they could do better and extended the tapings. Propelled by the songs on *Morrison Hotel*, the performances included gigs at New York City's Felt Forum and other venues on the East Coast and in the Midwest. Rothchild wanted *Absolutely Live* to be a stand-in for the Doors at their best—a concert for the ages.

Gloria Vanjak, reviewing the album for *Rolling Stone*, didn't believe it lived up to Rothchild's goal. She chastised Morrison for sounding "intoxicated" and flatly called out "Celebration of the Lizard" as "rancid." She saw little of value in the album, claiming, "What's theater on stage is garbage on the turntable." On Jim's drunken rant before "Break On Through," Vanjak said, "It's enough to make you want to get up and punch him."

Other reviewers, of course, didn't really talk about the album at all. Instead, they wrote about Miami and its consequences, which included increased concert security to keep Jim and the audience as far apart as possible. Without considering Jim's—and the band's—reality after Miami, Michael Bennett said in a widely syndicated article that during a recent show, the singer was "as mellow as Perry Como in front of a half-capacity audience." In short, most critics thought the Doors no longer mattered.

Released just five months after *Morrison Hotel*, the live record never approached its predecessor's sales. But bringing the *Roadhouse Blues* tour to life did capture the band's new bluesy strength. A highlight of the album is hearing the way Sixties audiences talked throughout the show and yelled during silent moments—unlike today, when everyone is too busy holding their phones and watching the little screen while filming.

Jim reacted by giving as good as he got, interacting with—and castigating— fans for yelling. At one point in "When the Music's Over," he screams "Shut up!" at the boisterous audience, then jokes in his Southern drawl: "Now, is that any way to behave at a rock-and-roll concert?" Less than a minute later, he let loose his "Now" scream as Ray shrieked behind him on the organ and Robby pounded out notes on his guitar. The fans erupted.

After the song ended and the cheering died down, Morrison told them they were "in for a special treat," clearly making light of Miami. Again, the crowd cheered loudly, recognizing the double meaning. Ray fake coughed behind him, and Jim joked:

No, no, not that. You only get that treat on full moons. Besides, I know there are a lot of young people out there, I wouldn't want you to faint. The last time it happened, grown men were weeping. Policemen were turning in their badges.

After Miami, the Doors were more restrained, but in *Absolutely Live* they demonstrated what they could still do, even if it was a tamer version. As Jim's banter with the fans proved, he was having fun onstage—despite FBI agents reporting on him, despite narcs spying on him from around every corner, and despite having to face an unfriendly media, who hadn't quite decided whether there was still a place at the table for a degenerate like Jim Morrison.

Although the album came out in July, everyone in the Doors was more concerned with the Miami trial set to begin on August 10. Officials in Florida wanted to make an example of the rock star, who was long a symbol of the counterculture. Jim stood on the precipice, looking at the strong possibility of doing hard time.

13
Another
Lost
Angel

The state of Florida killed Jim Morrison. The federal government was as an accomplice.

No, neither institution placed him in an electric chair or put him in front of a firing squad. Instead, Florida killed Morrison by unleashing an intensely political and cultural campaign to destroy him. The campaign against Jim was strategic and executed with precision.

First, the singer was silenced with manufactured charges that weren't filed for days after the fact. Then the Doors were stripped of their livelihood. The threat of real jail time exerted enormous pressure on Jim. In due course the burden accelerated his demise.

Soon the terror campaign against Morrison reached the office of President Richard Nixon, who applauded the work to bring down a leading agitator in the counterculture movement. Morrison represented what drove Nixon and his cronies mad. (In his letter to one of the student organizers of the Miami "Teenage Rally for Decency," Nixon thanked the young man for the "admirable initiative" to thwart "a number of critical problems confronting society.")

What Florida did to Morrison was criminal, an effort conceived of and carried out by a collection of thugs and crooks. That list of power brokers not only included Nixon, who watched greedily (and gleefully) from the sidelines, but also FBI Director J. Edgar Hoover, who lumped the Doors in with other agitators the federal government deemed "trash."

The insidious, malicious forces arrayed against Jim were determined to get him—and in the end they did. Insidiously and with malice, the weight of the state and federal government crushed Morrison, not only physically, but emotionally and existentially.

How did someone like Jim—committed to the antiauthoritarian impulses that ran rampant in his lifetime—fight a rigged system? Facing these odds, did he believe that he could win? Jim's close friend Ron Alain, who spent a lot of time with the singer, recalled:

> The Miami deal shook him up a bit. I remember we talked about that a few times, and it bugged him because they wanted to put him in jail. They wanted to make an example of him and put him away and take away his freedom.

"Getting Jim would have . . . put a dent in that [antiwar] movement, and that's what was going on," Densmore later said. Co-counsel Robert Josefsberg put it even more bluntly, calling Judge Murray Goodman "a coward," explaining, "he knew society was against Jim, but he was corrupted by his desire to stay in power."

What the pursuit of Morrison proved was that those in power weren't satisfied with his silence. They wanted his soul.

Between March 5, 1969, when acting police chief Paul Denham took warrants out on Jim, and the start of the trial on August 10, 1970, the federal government, the state of California, and the state of Florida tried several legal maneuvers to get the Doors front man to submit. At the same time, Jim's attorney, Max Fink, fought these efforts, including filing several motions to dismiss the case.

While the wrangling sped along, Morrison's personal life continued to unravel. He was arrested twice more in that seventeen-month span, first in November for causing a disturbance on a flight and then later the next August for public drunkenness in West Hollywood (when a sixty-eight-year-old woman found him sleeping on her porch and called the police). According to Manzarek, "Between Miami and Phoenix, Jim was facing a maximum of over thirteen years in prison."

Before the trial started, Jim had spent about three weeks in Paris between late June and late July 1970 in an attempt to prepare for the grueling ordeal ahead. More likely it was a way to release some of the pressure and distract himself from the negativity he faced back home. He could blend into the crowd in Europe in a way he could not in the United States. Reportedly, Jim was sick most of the trip, which included excursions to Spain and Morocco. When he got back to California, he stayed with Pam and recovered from a lingering bout of pneumonia.

When the trial finally began, all four Doors members were there. Robby sported a heavy beard and wore dark sunglasses. John looked on with a disgusted smirk. Ray stood defiant in a white sports coat and pants and thick muttonchops. Jim was all hair—a thick beard and a thick, long mane. It seemed that Jim was hiding, using his hair as camouflage. He had long before traded his leather pants for dark jeans and beat-up boots. He wore a white-striped, button-down shirt and a dark jacket. Morrison also carried his ever-present notebook. After looking at a stack of photographs from the night of the show, he joked with his bandmates and several friends outside the courtroom, "I'm beginning to believe I'm innocent."

Morrison's defense was based on the idea of artistic expression, particularly as it had transformed during the Sixties to include courser language and public nudity. Fink introduced a long list of books and films that put Jim's words in context of the era and the evolution of the First Amendment, which included movies like *Woodstock* (1970) and *I Am Curious (Yellow)* (1967) and novels such as John Updike's *Couples*, *The Godfather* by Mario Puzo, and Norman Mailer's *The Naked and the Dead*.

Co-counsels Fink and Josefsberg hoped to demonstrate that Jim's words and actions that night at the Key Auditorium may have been offensive to some but fell in line with the era's "community standards," a term that the defense team used repeatedly as a way to hammer it home to the six-person jury. Judge Goodman later denied the motion to enter the pop-culture material as evidence and ruled it "irrelevant" to the charges against Morrison. Goodman also limited the testimony of several people at the show that the defense hoped would prove Jim innocent.

Judge Goodman's rulings revealed all Jim needed to know about the supposed "fairness" of the trial. A journalist covering the trial said, "I can't escape the feeling that the transcript of the trial has already been written down somewhere, the verdict already decided and that we are all just going through the motions."

Josefsberg remembers that when the judge was preparing an order about the obscenity charge, he instructed the bailiff to take it out to the assembled media and journalists to get a feel for how it would be received. Such grandstanding for political gain, according to the attorney, proved Goodman had "no guts."

The judge played to the media, but there were other eyes on him. In the midst of an election year, he hoped to retain the seat he had been appointed to. Clearly, a conviction of a famous rock star would certainly have boosted his chances for reelection. "He knew society was against Jim," Josefsberg said. Morrison was a pawn in a larger battle for power.

The trial went on for forty days. The idea that prosecutors had to prove guilt beyond a reasonable doubt was gone. Morrison never had a chance even though the key piece of evidence was missing: No one had proof that Jim exposed himself. Even for those who swore he did, their distance from the stage would have made it impossible to really see anything. There were hundreds of photos from the show—not one proved a thing.

What Josefsberg remembered about Jim during the trial was his knowledge and attentiveness. "No client I ever had knew more about the criminal justice system," he recalled. "Jim understood what was going on." Addressing Morrison's mental and physical state, Josefsberg said Jim was "sober, clear-eyed, and focused."

When the defense tried to introduce additional testimony that showed Morrison didn't expose himself, Judge Goodman excused the jury, then told them, "Gentlemen, you've proven that Mr. Morrison didn't expose himself. I'm not going to allow this evidence to save time." The jury didn't hear that information, of course, before they made their decision.

Whether Morrison exposed himself was one thing, but the idea that he incited a riot or used language that was outside the bounds of what floated across popular culture in the 1960s made no sense. Calling what happened in Miami a "riot" was a stretch and surely no one could have believed that his use of expletives was worse than people had been hearing in other forms of media. The absurdity of the charges against him only deepened the notion that those in power were out to silence him. Morrison took the stand in an attempt to exonerate himself—which he didn't have to do—and was roundly praised for answering questions directly in his soft-spoken drawl. He wasn't the monster the prosecution made him out to be.

On September 18, Jimi Hendrix died in London, which Jim read about the next day, a Saturday morning. According to Hopkins and Sugerman, Morrison looked around and asked: "Does anyone believe in omens?"

After deliberating for much of September 19 and the morning of September 20, the jury returned a guilty verdict on the indecent exposure and open profanity charges, but not guilty on the felony charge of lewd and lascivious behavior and public drunkenness. Police officers escorted the singer to the Dade County Jail, trailed by a string of television cameras, reporters, and photographers. Later, speaking to the media, Jim explained: "This trial and its outcome won't change my style, because I maintain that I did not do anything wrong." In photos he looked bewildered and slightly dazed as he exited the courtroom.

Although he didn't spend time in jail following the guilty verdict, Morrison had been handcuffed and fingerprinted. Based on California's extradition laws, the judge increased his bond from five thousand to fifty thousand dollars (more than three hundred seventy-five thousand today). After paying the bond and huddling with Fink and Josefsberg, Jim was released.

Of Jim's reaction, Josefsberg recalled that he remained "very calm." He added: "Jim wasn't unkind, not to the security people or others coming in and out of the building. . . . He was kind and behaved . . . very nice—a decent human being."

On October 30, 1970, Jim Morrison was sentenced. The docket outlined that Jim was to "be imprisoned by confinement at hard labor in the Dade County Jail for a term of six months." His legal team appealed the decision immediately, which kept the singer free for the time being. Manzarek would later claim the Doors organization was committed to fighting the conviction up to the Supreme Court if necessary.

That is how you broke a butterfly on a wheel in the United States of America in 1970.

The weight of the verdict pulled Morrison apart. Before he was sentenced, his on-again, off-again friend Janis Joplin died. "You're drinking with number three," he reportedly told some friends. His world spiraled. Even Pam had had enough. She packed her bags and fled to Paris, reportedly to see a lover who was also one of her heroin dealers. The only hope for Jim—as always—seemed to be making music with the Doors.

While incarceration loomed, Jim and the band got back into the studio. Ray, Robby, and John understood the seriousness of the situation. Densmore claimed that saving Jim was the band's first priority: "Fuck, man, if we don't get an album or two more out of Jim, so what? Maybe we'll save his life." They thought the creative process would reverse the spiral. The strategy had worked with *Morrison Hotel.*

Ironically, the album that would later be named after their adopted home—*L.A. Woman*—would be made without longtime producer Paul Rothchild. He hated the songs the band planned to use for the new record, telling them, "It sucks . . . it's the first time I've ever been bored in a recording studio in my life." At a dinner, according to Hopkins and Sugerman, Rothchild told them that they should produce themselves with Botnick's assistance.

Although Rothchild may have disliked the tracks and sound, some felt that he still mourned Janis and was afraid to watch Jim's journey down a similar path toward destruction. He also wanted a more controlled sound and believed the band couldn't deliver, based on Jim's commitment to partying and the tension that it caused with Ray, Robby, and John.

Rothchild had a point. Krieger remembered Jim's drinking, saying, "When he got too drunk, he would become kind of an ass. It got harder and harder to be close with him." The band kind of lined up on one side—on the other, Jim and his increasing number of drinking buddies and hangers-on. In his memoir, Ray called them "reprobates . . . slime-balls, and general Hollywood trash."

Still, Botnick agreed to co-produce the next album, and the band went to work to perfect the demos and create several more. They set up shop at the Doors offices at 8512 Santa Monica Boulevard, which felt safe and secure for the band. With Jim across the street at the fleabag Alta Cienega Hotel, Robby remembered that the singer was reenergized by the process. Like the previous album, Botnick wanted to get a live feel. He said, "Go back to our early roots and try to get everything live in the studio with as few overdubs as possible."

Continuing the creative process that had worked on *Morrison Hotel,* the band wrote songs together, often from poems Jim had been working on over the years. Adding to the new vibe, they used Elvis's bassist Jerry Scheff and rhythm guitarist Marc Benno to add a deeper, more lush tone. Morrison sang in the adjoining bathroom to get the sound he wanted. To capture the desired live spirit, they didn't do many takes and kept over-dubs to a minimum.

Morrison's concept of *L.A. Woman* centered on imagining the city as a sexy woman, his way to pay homage to the "City of Lights." They also continued to explore what it meant to live on the West Coast and in the contemporary world. The sound was expansive, more alive than what they had done recently, despite the weight of Jim's conviction.

The title track "L.A. Woman," according to Densmore, epitomized the new sound, particularly Jim's anagram for his name. "'Mr. Mojo Risin' is a sexual term," the drummer explained. "I suggested that we slowly speed the track back up, kind of like an orgasm." For Robby, it was the teamwork that pulled the best work from the band. "The title track was distilled from jam sessions, with all of us contributing equally," he remembered. "Jim started with a handful of lines and added lyrics as he went while John kept it interesting with time changes and Ray and I harmonized on the melody and traded solos."

In 2022, the editors at *Bass Player* named the bassline of "L.A. Woman" one of the forty greatest of all time. "True to the production values of the day, Ray Manzarek's throbbing keyboard bass is all low frequencies and no mids, adding to its thunderous presence," they said. That unforgettable sound "takes everything that was best about The Doors—acid-drenched psychedelia, a threatening blues edge and that era-defining drone—and anchors it all with a rock-solid bassline." The enduring success of the song and its ranking among the best ever recorded is a demonstration of what the Doors could still create, particularly in their stripped-down, blues-infused era.

Despite the stress Jim experienced while putting the album together, the power of his vocals propelled the record. Morrison sounded lively— perhaps even sober—between takes. "I don't follow orders. I'm just a dumb singer," he playfully told his bandmates during one interval. Yet under Botnick's guiding hand, songs like "L.A. Woman" came together, as the producer explained, with "a little bit of woodshedding."

According to Robby, much of the beauty of "L.A. Woman" came from how he worked with Jim to bring the vocals and guitar into sync. "During the verses, I do these little answer lines to Jim's vocals. That was just a natural thing he and I would do. He'd sing something and I'd respond." The improvisation gave the song a timeless vibe, ramping up the power of the live feel. If you close your eyes, you can feel the sun on your face and hear the motor roaring as you're chugging down the Pacific Coast Highway. The glint off the ocean is blinding, but the air is clean, and the grit of the city is in the rearview mirror.

As a tribute to the great jazz pianist and composer Duke Ellington, Krieger wrote "Love Her Madly," whose title comes from the way the Duke ended his shows by telling audiences: "We love you madly!" It took the rest of the band, however, to work it into the Doors groove. "We workshopped it together," the guitarist said.

For the band, working collectively always worked best. "We tickled them and cajoled them and pampered them, and whipped them into line," Ray said of those tracks. "It was like the old days." *L.A. Woman* was a testament to that collaborative spirit.

Jim celebrated his twenty-seventh birthday on December 8 by recording some of his poetry, a longtime wish that he finally achieved. With some friends tagging along, Morrison spent four hours in the studio with a bottle of Irish whiskey and an engineer. By the end, he slurred his words as the alcohol kicked in. He was energized by what he got on tape.

Three days later the Doors played two sold-out shows at the State Fair Music Hall in Dallas. They were rusty and opened with "Love Her Madly," which would later be released as the first single off *L.A. Woman*. Journalist Gerry Barker said that Jim appeared "tired," explaining, "Much of the flair and flamboyance that used to mark him as the high priest of acid rock seemed gone." Hopkins and Sugerman countered that the band was excited by the power of the evening and did two encores at each performance. "Backstage after the second show," they said, "the four Doors toasted one another for the successful rally."

The Doors played their last concert together the next night on December 12 at the Warehouse in New Orleans. The thirty-five-hundred-seat hall on the banks of the Mississippi River was the top rock venue in the South. It had opened earlier in the year with a performance by the Grateful Dead. The San Francisco band's appearance in the Big Easy had been spoiled by a police raid at their hotel, which they later immortalized in the song "Truckin'." The famous line mentioned that they had been set up prior to the Bourbon Street arrest, "like a bowling pin."

The Warehouse gig was just as infamous for the Doors. According to a fan who saw the show, "Morrison was so loaded he could barely stand up. . . . They were terrible. . . . He was slurring and staggering."

What Densmore remembered was that the night before in Dallas they had debuted "Riders on the Storm," which went well. "Wow, we're going to be a cool rock-jazz group," he thought to himself. But "the next night Jim was so drunk it was terrible. I hated the erosion." During the show Morrison struggled, but he managed to play around with audience members who were lighting sparklers in the crowded hall.

Since the show was Jim's last, there's a mystique that surrounds the event. Ray famously claimed that Jim's "essence" left him while he stood on the stage in the voodoo city. The keyboardist equated this to Morrison's soul leaving his body. Disoriented, the singer forgot his lyrics and sat down on the drum riser and barely moved. When he finally got back up—allegedly with help from Densmore's boot—he grabbed the microphone stand and beat it into the stage until it broke a hole in the wooden floor. They finished the set with "The End" and never performed together again.

There are several versions of what happened that last night. One is that John was so disgusted that he stood up, threw his drumsticks, and stormed off the stage. Another is that the three Doors walked off, leaving Morrison by himself onstage as the house lights came on. George Friedman, the Warehouse stage manager, provided a different perspective, writing that Jim was definitely drunk ("whacked near a stupor that night"), but, at the end of the show, he "suddenly jumped up, grabbed the microphone and then smashed it right through the floor of the stage." Friedman said: "What an ending to a great show . . . the music indeed was over when they turned out the lights and the Doors left the stage."

The Doors agreed to stop touring after New Orleans. Jim worked on a variety of projects, including his poetry, some films, and more or less reunited with Pam when she came back from Paris. Hopkins and Sugerman note, however, that his drinking had ramped up: "Only the end was invariable: total inebriation."

In early March 1971, Jim told Ray, Robby, and John that he was leaving for Paris to start anew with Pam and transition to a different life away from the rock-star world he had created. "We unanimously agreed that Paris would be a good thing for Jim," Krieger remembered. "A chance to relax and put the pressures of the world and the band behind him . . . to center himself and come back with a renewed passion for making music." The guitarist viewed the respite as a way for the singer to renew his passion for performing.

"Love Her Madly," the first single from the new record had debuted, climbing to number eleven on the *Billboard* chart and number seven on *Cashbox*. The song's success gave the band high hopes for the album, even if they weren't touring.

In April, Elektra released *L.A. Woman*. The album reached number nine on the *Billboard* album chart and then remained in the top two hundred for thirty-six weeks. Later, in June, "Riders on the Storm" came out as a single and eventually hit number fourteen.

Before he left for France, Jim gave an impromptu interview to Ben Fong-Torres, an editor at *Rolling Stone*. The singer explained that the Doors were "at a crossroads of our career," particularly since young audiences wanted new music by new bands, not an "anachronism" like their group. He spoke of making movies and other interests that didn't include the Doors.

Jim arrived in Paris on June 12, 1971. He went to Pam's room at the Hotel George V, which he likened to a whorehouse. She wasn't there. Before long he was across the street, reportedly drinking whiskey—one after another.

One morning John answered the phone. It was Jim calling from abroad. He wanted to find out how *L.A. Woman* was doing. Densmore told him how the first single had become a hit and that the album was getting a lot of airplay. Jim replied, "I'll be back and we'll do some more."

Three weeks later he would be dead.

Whether Jim was already far too gone when he left for Paris or not, he died under mysterious circumstances on July 3, 1971, at 17 rue Beautreillis. He had lit a fuse just six years earlier on a beach in Santa Monica, and the dynamite finally exploded.

For the next several decades, various investigators, journalists, and others would attempt to figure out how and why Morrison died. But when his longtime lover Pam Courson died three years later, any hope for determining the truth likely went with her.

What we have left is speculation and educated guesses. Jim may have accidentally overdosed, allegedly snorting heroin and/or cocaine in the bathroom of a seedy Paris drug den that fronted as a nightclub. He could have done drugs with Pam in their apartment and died with or without her knowledge. She was hooked on heroin, but Jim hated needles, so there's little chance that he injected himself.

There is also a simple possibility—that Jim died of a heart attack brought on by alcohol addiction and stress. He was also at least 40 pounds overweight, which could have contributed to his heart giving out.

Most people believe that a twenty-seven-year-old man could not have possibly drank himself to death, even someone with Morrison's prodigious habits. However, according to several addiction counselors and recovering alcoholics, that outcome makes sense. Even if he had lived past the trauma of that evening, the alcohol would have eventually killed him. What separated Jim from many other performers—and elevated him to icon status like Dylan—was his authenticity. Krieger saw that gig after gig, explaining, "When you went to see a Doors show, you saw the real Jim Morrison. There was no difference between Jim on- or offstage. But the magic of Jim is that Jim was just . . . Jim. The audience may not have known Jim personally, but on some level they could sense that he was being genuine." Similarly, Dylan was transformed into a living, breathing symbol of the Sixties, because his integrity was held up as an example of how to champion love and compassion in a time when the state machine forced the world into warfare and depravity.

The many sides of Morrison are essential in thinking about him and his legacy—the total complexity of a life. He once defined the word *hero* for a reporter, again allowing us to peek inside his mind. "A hero rebels against the facts of existence and seems to conquer them . . . it can't be a lasting thing."

What Jim Morrison achieved in his life was a way to become immortal, despite the cost. There are not many people who continue to have consequence long after they're gone.

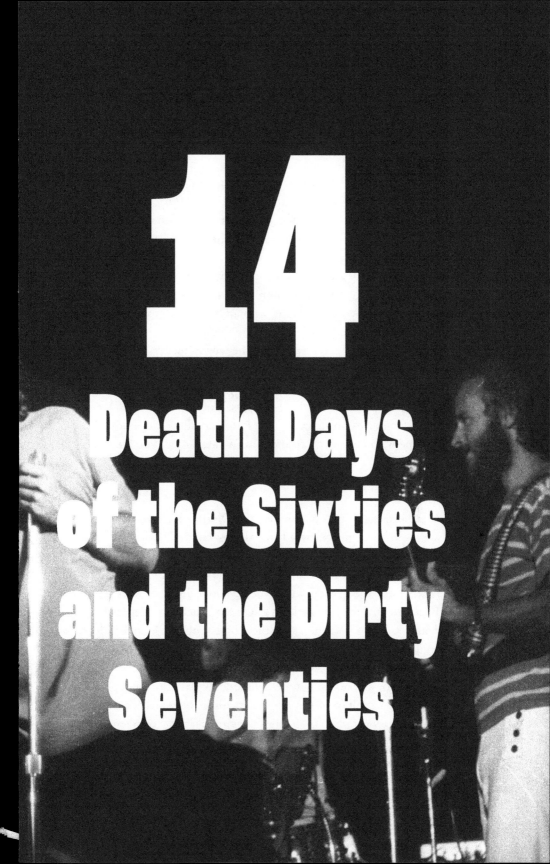

14

Death Days of the Sixties and the Dirty Seventies

Attorney Robert Josefsberg walked to the witness stand in the Dade County Courtroom. All eyes were on his client—Jim Morrison. As co-counsel for the defense, one of Josefsberg's main jobs was to interview potential jurors who might serve in the case the state of Florida had built against Morrison.

Jim's team had determined that the best path for defending the singer was to show that his actions at the Miami concert were in the bounds of his First Amendment rights. But the gap between the counterculture and the rest of America was laid bare by the attorney's line of questioning.

Josefsberg approached several older women who were in the juror pool. When the lawyer asked them "what their attitude was about the use of the four-letter word beginning with an 'F,'" he later recalled, "a couple little old ladies passed out."

Remember: this is August 1970. The word "fuck" was so provocative that these women couldn't handle hearing about it in an open forum. Josefsberg never actually said fuck—he just hinted at it.

Now, think about the Sixties—hippies, Woodstock, protest, Vietnam—a flood of memories or images of news footage, films, or photos. Compare that scene with the Miami courtroom. Whatever gap you see, multiply it.

Manzarek and Morrison founded the Doors to create a portal into a new type of perception, based on Aldous Huxley's book *The Doors of Perception*, published in 1954. From the outside, however, Morrison and the other members of the band can help us understand the magnitude of the Sixties and the new decade of the Seventies. In other words, the Doors can be used as a lens for looking at the era. Their experiences help us see it clearer and give us context for the whole scope of American history, in fact, including the country's present and future.

We also need to scrutinize the era through the lens of Vietnam—because there was nothing more consequential at that time. Jim's life, for example, is a symbol of the reaction against the war because he had to turn on his own father, a lifelong Navy officer who commanded an aircraft carrier during the war. Like many other families across the United States, the Morrison household was divided.

Rich Linnell, Doors roadie and member of the band's inner circle, separated them from the straightforward antiwar groups that sprang to life in San Francisco. "It was an important time for people to explore, to resist the old ways and to challenge and come up with new ways of thinking." The Doors' new sound, then, served as a model for people seeking a different path. In several songs, like "Five to One" and "The Unknown Soldier," they were direct, but none of the band members spearheaded the movement.

If you think about the Sixties—the hippie era—as a decade based on ideas of peace, equality, and love, then the young people who powered it were far ahead of those in power, whose thinking and ideas were outdated. For those who had power, it was inconceivable that capitalism and democracy might fall at the hands of demonstrators, activists, and people from different racial and ethnic backgrounds. So those in power used formal institutions to suppress dissidents and attempts at insurrection.

What the Doors and other bands asked was whether there could be change. Looking at the Rolling Stones and the Doors specifically, they pushed the limit of what the system considered acceptable resistance. As the system deemed each group suspect, each group had to be suppressed. For the Stones, they fought back with album titles such as *Their Satanic Majesties Request* (1967) and *Let It Bleed* (1969) and a move toward a more aggressive sound as they moved into the Seventies.

According to historian Bryan Burrough, "A revolution was arriving, but it was a cultural rather than a political phenomenon." Bob Dylan led the way for the groups that followed and helped people see that music could serve the revolution. The Beatles took the power of music and its messages to a global audience. Jagger and Morrison gave darkness a central role. Change needed a sharp edge that hinged on more than love and peace. How else could the next "Street Fighting Man" emerge: "'Cause summer's here and the time is right for fighting in the street, boy." This is the same person that Morrison screamed wanted the world—now!

Putting 1968 into context, cultural historian Greil Marcus explained, "The feeling that the country was coming apart—that, for what looked and felt like a casually genocidal war in Vietnam, the country had committed crimes too great they could not be paid." Instead, he said, "The country deserved to live out its time in its own ruins." Marcus's "dread" of 1968 overshadowed even the presidential election, despite its role in cementing the power of Nixon's conservative "silent majority."

For Marcus, however, the Doors stood apart. They projected an aura of dread—"A group of people who appeared to accept the present moment at face value." The Doors engaged the souls of their listeners and gave them what they had at their core: "mistrust" and "doubt." The Doors radiated contempt, which came from Morrison and made him a more dangerous guide for America's youth than his contemporaries. As Krieger noted, "He was totally committed to living the life of the revolution."

Both the Baby Boomer generation and the Vietnam War are deeply complicated topics that historians and writers are still attempting to figure out. On one hand, the war and the demonstrations against it colored everything that would follow for the Boomers, including their march to power as they aged. According to author Bruce Cannon Gibney, they used their size and voting power to run "amok" and game the system in their favor. "A plague of generational locusts," Gibney concludes. The Boomers really did want the world, as Morrison sang. But he would have never imagined the way they later defiled that concept.

Looking at the data on young people's thoughts on the war does little to make the picture clearer. The Sixties generation really was divided on Vietnam for much of the decade. According to Gibney, Gallup polls demonstrated that most young people supported the war until the latter half of 1968. Before that date, college-educated young men (aged eighteen to twenty-four) supported Johnson's war more than all other demographic segments. The schism between what occurred at the time and how the Boomers *remembered* Vietnam—and spread its messages throughout popular culture—is confounding at best and damning at worst.

As popular culture increasingly defined the war and its era, it seemed everyone was against Vietnam, had marched in the streets, and risked life and limb to fight for the righteous cause of peace. While real-life Vietnam veterans were battling against ideas that they were all murderers and baby killers, they were portrayed in popular movies like *The Deer Hunter* (1978) and *Apocalypse Now* (1979), which were released just a few years after the fall of Saigon, in ways that furthered the stereotype.

In the 1980s filmmakers used the Vietnam War, and the cultural rifts it incited, in movies that tacitly questioned the foreign-policy moves of President Ronald Reagan. Like many pundits and critics, they saw a similarity between the earlier conflict and America's becoming the world's police force. The real-life war in Southeast Asia took on an additional role and gave authors, artists, and commentators a tool to question current diplomacy.

As the Boomers extended their influence across all of American culture, Vietnam remained a focal point and served as a guiding principle for Boomer presidents like Bill Clinton and George W. Bush. The idea was that every American military intervention had to be seen through the lens of Vietnam—the eternal question of *quagmire* was ever-present. The mistreatment of veterans who returned from Southeast Asia also looms and fuels scorn-filled nationalism among conservatives today who use the phrase "Support Our Troops" as a rallying cry for dogmatic acceptance of right-wing doctrine.

The fuzzy logic of what happened in the Sixties and how it unraveled in the Seventies even extended to drug use among troops in Vietnam. According to historian James Wright, "the stakes were too high out in the field" for drug use to match what people perceived (excessive drug use would be another pop-culture driver in the Seventies through today). According to one vet Wright interviewed, being stoned while fighting "would have been suicide."

Like Morrison, troops preferred alcohol. Some used it to give them strength to fight against future horrors; others needed it to let off steam. The atrocities some American troops committed deepened the animosity between soldiers on one side and protesters on the other, who bought into the stereotype of them as drunken, drug-addled troops hell-bent on enacting a cowboys-and-Indians vision of the war.

From late 1968 through the late Seventies, people grappled with many conflicting ideas that complicated the nation's collective memory of Vietnam. In the 1970s Vietnam vets were often whispered about as "crazy" or, it was implied, "were still fighting Vietnam in their minds." Some people were simply "never right in the head again after serving" or "had seen friends die." Prominent was the guilt people felt for the vets, but also the feeling that they were too far gone to help.

According to Wright, "Families and friends ignoring Vietnam was often the result of a tacit mutual agreement: Let's forget about this last year." At the heart of the challenge with reestablishing a postwar culture was the inability to communicate: "Most men were not eager to discuss the war experience with those who had not been there. They were not sure how to describe or explain it—and, in fact, many veterans have spent years trying to make sense of their experiences." Popular culture kept the picture muddy because, when it came to the era, audiences had mixed feelings and memories. That relentless push to reimagine the war and its consequences lasted deep into the Seventies—and, arguably, will continue until the Boomers are long gone from positions of power.

It can also be argued that the gap between those who served in Vietnam (80 percent from disadvantaged backgrounds) and those who got deferments cemented the demographic distinctions today between the upper 20 percent and everyone else. Deferments, Gibney explains, "became an exercise of class privilege, and, given the overrepresentation of minorities among the poor, of racial discrimination." We are still attempting to break down these barriers that the Boomers continued to fortify as they gained real economic and political power from the Seventies onward.

Vietnam remains a difficult subject to assess, and few answers are concrete. One perspective centers on the extremely personal viewpoint. The war and its consequences destroyed lives, not only for those killed and their families, but in the way the war in Southeast Asia warped the nation's moral fabric. Rather than wrangle with the difficult aspects of the Sixties and Vietnam (because it forces you to contemplate extremely difficult issues and imagery), people resort to the pop-culture view of the era and war—heavy on melodrama and nostalgia. Countless millions of people have seen *Forrest Gump*, but how many people have actually considered the real lives lost in Vietnam or the global devastation the war generated?

"[1960s America] was beyond our imaginations, it was more dramatic, more surrealistic, more fanciful, more incredible, more vivid, than anything we would have dared to write about."
—Norman Mailer

As remarkable as it may seem, *Time* magazine named Richard Nixon "Man of the Year" in 1971 and 1972. Two years later he resigned in disgrace because of the bungled Watergate burglary and his attempts at covering it up. As a result, Americans almost universally place Vietnam and Watergate in the same mental category. We compartmentalize events and put them in order to make them easier to understand, but that mental trick dampens the real sense of how historical episodes unfold.

Yet the scandals and violence of the late Sixties and Seventies affected the Boomer generation as they took power. That they would take it was never in doubt, but what mattered was what they would do with it.

For literary critic Morris Dickstein, the "magnitude" of stress represented by the violence in Vietnam and the massacres at Kent State and Jackson State in 1970 told the Boomers—consciously or subconsciously—that the spirit of the 1960s got crushed by the weight of the war, capitalism, and a corrupt government. As a result, a generation of apparent peaceniks and activists gave way to the rise of the perfect consumeristic machine. Dickstein explained: "Losing its political bearings in an era of economic strain, the counterculture of the Sixties turned into the narcissistic Me Generation of the 1970s and the ambitious, self-involved young professionals of the 1980s."

By the mid-Seventies, the Doors were long gone. They released two post-Morrison albums—*Other Voices* (1971) and *Full Circle* (1972)—that did little to keep them viable. During the next several years the music business would shed its Sixties hippie vibe and confront a world that seemed more realistic and unforgiving—the kind of place the Doors had taken the culture during their heyday. In 1975 Dylan reemerged with *Blood on the Tracks* (1975), a darker, Doors-like examination of a harsher world. Greil Marcus called the new album "dark, pessimistic, and discomforting."

The Rolling Stones emerged from the tragedy of Altamont with the classic Seventies albums *Sticky Fingers* (1971) and *Exile on Main St.* (1972), which had followed the two great albums that closed out the previous decade, *Beggars Banquet* (1968) and *Let It Bleed* (1969). This evolution turned the Stones into the most important band in the world and symbolized the death of the Sixties and rise of the dirty Seventies.

If Altamont symbolized the end of the Sixties, then we can measure the pulse the 1970s through the Stones' themes of violence, drug use, consumerism, and the coke-fueled, disco-filled late 1970s and early 1980s. No one else on the rock scene could have created the psychedelic, Beatles-inspired *Satanic Majesties* and also *Emotional Rescue* (1980) and *Tattoo You* (1981). If Morrison had lived and the band stayed together, who knows what kind of direction they would have taken—a path similar to Mick and Keith or maybe they would have ended up a jazz-infused disco band with Jim in leather leisure suits.

Forty years after Jim was convicted in a Dade County courtroom, Florida Governor Charlie Crist granted Morrison a pardon. While this symbolic act was just another news story for the national media, it represented something important.

Attorney Robert Josefsberg spoke about Morrison specifically, but he could have been atoning for everyone who lived through the era, saying, "I'm very pleased he's been pardoned, maybe his soul will rest more peacefully now." The lawyer, only five years older than Jim, remembered, "Contrary to the image . . . he was kind, considerate. He was sober and he had a great sense of humor . . . a very decent person."

Josefsberg's words—which contrast image versus reality—serve us well in thinking about Jim as well as the Sixties. "The whole country was polarized," John Densmore explained, looking back at the end of the decade. "It was 'for the war' or 'against the war.'"

15

Resurrection of the Lizard King

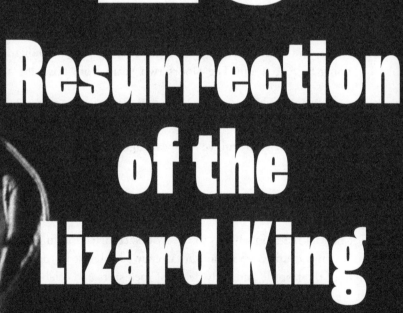

Jim Morrison's 1971 death ended the band as a foursome—the trio put out the two albums afterward and allegedly even considered Paul McCartney as a replacement—but Jim's passing gave rise to Morrison as rock god, as myth, and as a forever-young rebel who pushed against society's limits. That iconic status, conferred by fans and driven by the Doors as a corporate/business entity, remains strong.

If the early years of the 2020s can be used to forecast the future of Morrison and the Doors, all indicators show that the band is as popular as ever. Both Robby and Jim had recent best-selling books: Krieger's long-awaited memoir and Jim's opus, *The Collected Works of Jim Morrison*.

No one, certainly not the remaining Doors, could have predicted the future back in 1971.

"I thought after the last album, and then Jim passing away, I thought, nobody's going to care about The Doors two years from now. It's all over."
—Robby Krieger

"It's like some psychedelic dream we had years ago; we're still in it."
—John Densmore

The major factors that contributed to the Doors' resurrection in the first decade after Jim's death were radio and a renewed interest in the singer as a symbol of the fast life and early death of rock stars and celebrities.

Today we might think that Morrison's rise to icon happened right away, but, looking back, it took time to spark. For example, the band released *The Best of the Doors* in 1973 and the collection more or less fizzled. In comparison, the 1980 album *The Doors Greatest Hits* exploded and ultimately sold two million copies. Those records would also be handed from friend to friend and traded among younger brothers and sisters, which infused the band into the Gen-X ethos.

When Ray, Robby, and John decided to put Jim's poetry to music and released *An American Prayer* in 1978, the public—and radio deejays—began to take note. Suddenly, the Doors seemed new again in the seven years since Jim's death. Rock radio catapulted the band in the sweep against disco and pop music and was kept fresh by new bands whose music was in the same vein as the Doors.

A year later, Francis Ford Coppola used "The End" in his film *Apocalypse Now*. It played at the beginning of the movie and seemed like it was its theme song. The opening scene, featuring attack helicopters against a deep burnt orange sky, became a haunting part of popular-culture legend. The result, according to Elektra founder Jac Holzman, proved the Doors were "a band with relevance . . . people understood from hearing the material again that that lean, clean, very spare musical line that they had did not put the music into any time zone. The music was itself timeless." The idea of timelessness was new in the late Seventies and Eighties. Not many bands or performers had earned that designation, particularly in an era before technology gave people wide access to music from the past.

Ironically, Coppola had gone to UCLA film school with Morrison and Manzarek, so the band sent him an older version of the song to use in the soundtrack that was slightly different from the one on their debut album. The film took the Doors to new audiences across America and around the world and made more than a hundred million dollars (about four hundred million dollars today).

While the album and movie were important, the true catalyst for the band's resurrection was the book *No One Here Gets Out Alive* by Jerry Hopkins and Danny Sugerman. Although it was initially rejected dozens of times by publishers (who thought no one would be interested in a dead rock star), Sugerman's insider status and some tinkering by Ray Manzarek gave the manuscript a boost. The result was more than a biography but an instant classic in rock-music history. It might be impossible to make either of two important calculations. First, how many copies of *No One* were passed around and read over and over by a generation of eager readers? (Say, those primarily born as early as 1955 and through the late 1960s.) Second, we'll never be able to fully weigh the book's impact on Jim's elevation to cult status—if it's possible for a rock star and his biography to be considered *cult* when they are so utterly mainstream.

The early Eighties push continued when *Rolling Stone*—one of the few sources of hipness before cable television really blossomed—put Morrison on the cover with the provocative title: "Jim Morrison. He's hot, he's sexy and he's dead." Inside were the stories of a new generation of Morrison fans (presented as kind of infantile and fatuous) obsessed with the dead singer's "mystique." According to Bryn Bridenthal, a spokesperson at Elektra, the Doors sold more albums in 1980 than any year since the debut in 1965, and some albums sold two or three times more versus the previous year. John Densmore told the story of a friend who said to him, "Shit, you guys are famous again."

While renewed media attention led to Morrison's appeal to younger fans, it was the millions of daily classic-rock radio listeners who fueled the phenomenon. Back in the 1980s, when you could call a major radio program on the phone and make a personal request, countless fans were demanding the Doors, right along with Van Halen, AC/DC, and Cheap Trick. In fact, the same marketing machines that were pushing these new bands were also keeping the Doors in front of listeners. The Eighties was an age of mythologizing every type of hero or antihero. Morrison, who could fit either category depending on your outlook, fit perfectly into the era.

While countless people were simultaneously engaged in hero worship when it came to rock stars, the effort felt communal, individual, and immediate. *I* could love the Doors, while *we* could celebrate their music by picking up a new compilation album or talking about our favorite parts of Hopkins and Sugerman's *No One Here Gets Out Alive*. Your best friend could choose the Rolling Stones over the Doors or the Beatles, but you could both celebrate in the hedonism and allure of Mick and Jim. As writer Steven Hyden said of his own experience, "They were like gods, who I secretly believed could elevate my own humdrum existence if I had enough faith in the classic-rock mythos."

For Hyden and others, Morrison—the person, but more important the myth—gave you license to act out, pushing our own version of rebellion. He blamed Morrison for "all that time I spent in my twenties staring vainly into barroom mirrors while I drank and drugged myself into oblivion . . . I should've known better." He explained: "The Lizard King was too ingrained in my psyche. I wanted to ride the snake, man, and got off on watching myself break on through to the other side." This same mindset replicated itself countless times every weekend across the country throughout the Eighties and Nineties.

The huge success of Hopkins and Sugerman's book certainly fueled some of the mythology. Regardless of whether the authors intended it, readers gravitated to the book's most outrageous stories and anecdotes, which turned Morrison into a wild child and angst-ridden soul who couldn't fulfill his aspirations as a poet, which then set off a headlong dive into drugs and booze.

Even the book's cover seemed to turn Jim into a kind of whiskey-addled Superman, an illustration of the famous young-lion photo with Morrison outlined in bright yellow-orange with a red background. He is at once sinister and angelic, his Adonis-like features are darkened (along with intensified chest hair), and there is an almost religious ambiance from the halo effect. The illustration creates a figure who is slightly more muscular than in real life, as well as more menacing—serious and mysterious.

Morrison becomes the ideal personification of the boyfriend or best friend, the ultimate bad boy, way too cool for any of us to really understand. I grew up in a town that was so small that it didn't have a public library, but, in the larger city nearby, the copies of No One were constantly stolen. An underground network sprung to life to get the book into our hands. Many dog-eared copies were passed from teen to teen.

Given its status as the first biography of Morrison, there is no way to underestimate the book's importance in understanding Jim and his bandmates—that is, at least from the perspective of the two authors. Over the years, each of the remaining Doors expressed doubts about how events were characterized in the book and the overall portrait it painted of the singer. Reading it now, it's hard to imagine that some of the countless quotes and episodes weren't embellished, particularly some of Jim's words that could only have been remembered by him. Personally, I'm at war with myself over how to perceive No One today. It is both undoubtedly monumental and somewhat flawed.

As a fan of creative nonfiction, I find the book eminently readable and entertaining. Yet it also drew a great deal of criticism for implying that Jim may have faked his death. In the ensuing years, Hopkins has written at length about the book, which includes the notion that he wanted the publisher to print half the versions with that ending and half with Morrison dying in Paris.

The most interested reader of Hopkins and Sugerman may have been acclaimed film director Oliver Stone. The book was a primary source document for his film *The Doors* (1991), a biopic starring Val Kilmer as Morrison. Most people, especially Doors aficionados, have strong feelings about the film with little middle ground. For those who enjoyed it, the movie was an encapsulation of all they loved about Jim and the band. Detractors, however, saw it as exploitation and a caricature of the singer to fit a Hollywood narrative that reduced Morrison to his basest moments.

Several decades later, the idea that jumps out is that the Morrison from *The Doors*, though played brilliantly by Kilmer, was too one-sided. As a result, the depiction played it safe, as if the exploration wasn't the key to creating a robust character. Oddly, that vibrancy was what seemed to be Stone's most powerful tool—for example, Chris Taylor (Charlie Sheen) in *Platoon* (1986) or Gordon Gekko (Michael Douglas) in *Wall Street* (1987).

The harshest critics of Stone's film were the remaining members of the Doors. Each took shots at the director for mangling Jim, basically turning him into a drunken, hedonistic lout. The counterargument was that Manzarek, in particular, hoped to someday make his own film and that Stone beat him to it, thereby ruining his chances. Robby was the least antagonistic about *The Doors* film but still criticized Stone for its "disservice to Jim." He explained:

> He came across as a pretentious, obnoxious, stupid drunk who was a dick to everyone around him. I'm not saying he wasn't a drunk, and I'm not saying he couldn't be obnoxious at times. But he wasn't blitzed twenty-four hours a day with a bottle of Jack in his hand, screaming about death. He was funny, and shy, and when he was out of line he knew it, and he was sorry. He had a way of making everyone who met him feel like he was their best friend.

The biggest challenge, Krieger explained, was that the blending of fact and fiction gradually gets taken as truth: "Oliver Stone's movie is laughable as a historical artifact, but parts of it have seeped into the official record."

Oliver Stone's film was his latest in a series of attempts to reformulate contemporary American history, including *Platoon*, *Wall Street*, *Born on the Fourth of July* (1989), and *JFK* (1991). In the early 2010s, Stone would star in and direct a documentary series called *The Untold History of the United States*, which led to an extensive lecture tour and best-selling book.

If there were a near-universal feeling about *The Doors*, it was applause for Kilmer's portrayal of the Lizard King. Jac Holzman claimed he was "terrific" in the role and "magical" in re-creating the energy and excitement of the band's gigs at the Whisky. Even Krieger agreed, saying that he thought the actor deserved an Academy Award for the performance.

In his later memoir, Kilmer wrote at length about his process—extremely physical and requiring absolute concentration—of getting the role correct. Both Paul Rothchild and Robby Krieger were shocked at his transformation into Morrison to the point that at different times working with him they forgot that Kilmer *wasn't* Jim.

The strange tragedy of *The Doors*, however, is that Kilmer had the vulnerability and sensitivity to play all aspects of Morrison. In other words, he could have given the critics what they wanted, *if* Stone would have given him the space to do so. By the end of the production, Kilmer was spent. "I felt like I had experienced glory. Nirvana," he remembered. "And what next? To live or die? What would life look like, pretending to be normal after getting a taste of heaven? After touching the pearly gates?" He would go on to play several phenomenal characters, including Doc Holliday in *Tombstone* (1993), but his instinct was correct.

"Jim and I were pretty close in age, and we kind of hit [it] off. He was a very nice person. I've seen the movie about him and the Doors. Oliver Stone, with all due respect, is a revisionist. In the movie Jim was portrayed as a selfish druggie, and he wasn't. He was a very nice person, a nice, decent human being with a very good sense of humor. We spent a lot of time with notepads, passing notes back and forth to each other, and he was very perceptive, very bright. He understood everything going on around him. And for the three weeks I was with him, he was sober."

—Robert Josefsberg, co-counsel during the Miami trial

Two years after the Stone film, the Doors were inducted into the Rock & Roll Hall of Fame. The event brought the band's resurrection full circle—because what has remained the backbone of the rebirth is the music they created.

The only challenge in being a Doors fan, however, is keeping up with the amount of music they have released. The steady flow makes it seem like they are still recording and makes one wonder how much more there could be in various archives and vaults. For example, there have been three live albums, which came out in 1983, 1987, and 1991. But the number of archival compilations reaches nearly twenty-five. Starting with 1970's *13*, there have been another twenty compilations and eight boxed sets.

On Spotify the band has nearly nine million monthly listeners, about the same as Bob Dylan. Comparatively, Led Zeppelin has more than sixteen million, the Stones are at twenty-one million, and the Beatles twenty-six million.

While these figures might indicate some softness in the popularity of the Doors, when ChartMasters analyzed total sales and streaming across all platforms, it determined that the debut album stands as the most popular of any year from its release through 1969, even surpassing *Sgt. Pepper's*.

"Nobody played drums like John Densmore, nobody played keyboards like Ray Manzarek, and nobody sang like Jim Morrison. I had my own thing going, too. Put us together and we sounded like ourselves. We were the Doors."

—Robby Krieger

No discussion of Doors-related mythmaking is complete without talking about the role that Ray, Robby, and John played in its construction. A caveat, however, before castigating any of them—they were young men when Morrison passed away. Not only did they have to weigh their own relationships with their dead friend and the six short years they were together as a band, but they then had to spend the rest of their lives talking about that era and one another.

Just about every group that has ever had a hit record will eventually tell stories about how they come to hate the song. Can you imagine how confining it might have been for Ray, Robby, and John to be stuck together for their adult lives, in addition to living with the weight of Jim's immortality? Whatever level of guilt they carried as human beings—particularly as our thinking about addiction and recovery has transformed—their friend floats above them. Morrison's death made them wealthier too, which may have intensified their remorse.

Over the years the pressures on them led to private spats and public outrages. The Doors would become "The Doors of the 21st Century." There would be accusations of *what Jim would have wanted*, battles with the heirs to the Morrison estate, and much wrangling over what it meant to be a Door—back then and well into the current century. As creative individuals, they knew that, no matter what they did, they would never approach what they achieved in that short, four-year window between 1967 and 1971.

In his memoir, Robby explained, "The source of so many Doors myths can be traced back to Ray, and he went so deep with it that he convinced himself of some of his bullshit." He admitted that Manzarek even doubted that Jim was dead after one of their visits to his grave: "He's not in there, man. I can tell." Krieger is also a realist and admitted that Ray's efforts paid off. "A new generation was discovering our legend. More importantly: they were discovering our music."

John, who publicly seems to be the Door who mellowed the most as he aged, placed the band and Jim's role onto a higher plane, writing, "His three musical sidekicks (and it took three of us to match the energy of this one person) were lucky (and talented enough) to figure out the perfect sound bed for Jim to lie down in." Densmore also admitted that it took him many years to work through his grief and anger toward Morrison.

In 2011, writer Jon Friedman called Morrison "a vivid presence in the minds of his fanatical fans." The word *fanatical*—defined as "excessive and single-minded zeal"—seemed instructive. The group's popularity has always been fueled by fans and listeners who can't get enough of a very specific moment-in-time version of the Doors: Jim's wild-lion look and Manzarek's idiosyncratic organ work as expressed at the beginning of "Light My Fire."

Yet there is no single answer to why the Doors remain so alive to us today, more than fifty years since they catapulted into the national consciousness in the summer of 1967. That mysticism is part of the allure. Like another American classic—F. Scott Fitzgerald's 1925 novel *The Great Gatsby*—the Doors have been many things to listeners over that time, but they have been incessantly reinterpreted for each new era, just like the character of Jay Gatsby and that alluring green light at the end of the dock.

Even in the mid-Sixties, the Doors were hard to pin down. Were they a blues-rock band, a pop group with a dark edge, or something completely new? They were certainly not the era's typical Los Angeles band riding the wave of artsy folk tunes or surf-city vibes, although "I Looked at You" on their debut album sounds like a close relative to the 1962 Beach Boys classic "Surfin' Safari" (perhaps the closest Jim and the band got to a California sound. . . ."And we're on our way . . .").

Jimmy Greenspoon, a keyboardist who made it big with Three Dog Night, was on the scene before the Doors became popular. Back then, he remembered, they were "a best kept secret . . . but there was nothing like them." Rather than categorize them, Greenspoon explained, "We didn't hear what they did as 'pop' or 'psychedelic'; it was just intense and brooding . . . the Doors were just heavier than anybody around."

Talking to Baby Boomers who were teens at the time the Doors hit the national stage, a slightly different picture emerges with two distinct alternatives. Most fans back then seemed to either have outright love for the band's dark, artsy sound; or, as one woman (who was seventeen years old in 1967) exclaimed, "That was druggie music!" Love/hate, nothing in between.

Jac Holzman, who launched it all by signing the band, explained: "There's never been a band quite like them or a band that will last as long into the future as I think the Doors will. I think people will always find something of relevance in the Doors."

Jim Morrison would be approaching eighty today. We may be able to contextualize that idea—take a look at Mick and Keith or Dylan and imagine what might have been. Many Sixties rock stars are still on the scene playing their hits, and a few are even making new music.

Yet we don't actually have to. In our mind's eye, there is a picture— maybe it's the young man in tight leather pants, or maybe it's Morrison with a full beard in a brown buckskin jacket, the portrait of the artist struggling with who he was. But we have that image; it's there and clear as can be.

Then, there's the voice—also vibrant and bold. Maybe it's paired with Ray's bassline and carnivalesque organ or a Krieger solo. Again, we hear it. Sometimes we never forget it.

"Gonna have a realllaaa, ahh good time."

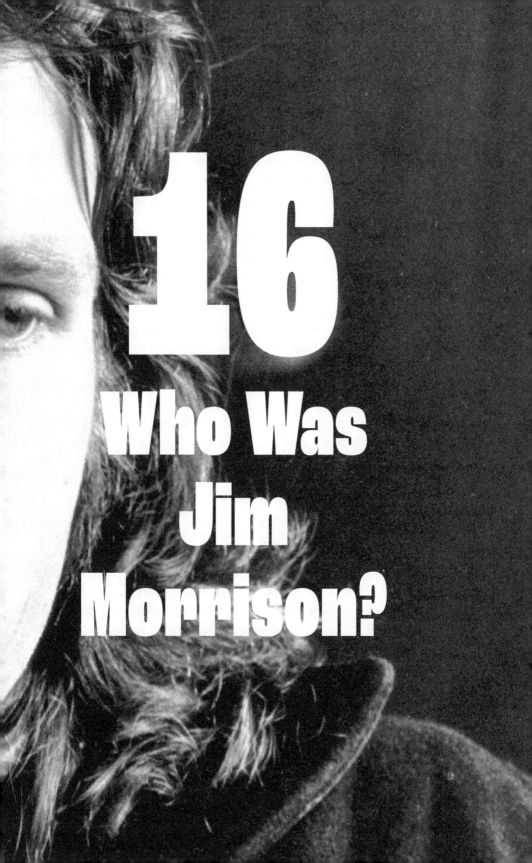

16
Who Was Jim Morrison?

At two vastly different points in my life—one as a reckless grad student facing down a slew of personal demons, the other as a thirtysomething, cleaned-up professional—I met two women who had dated Jim Morrison. They were both acquaintances who knew that I was a Doors fan, but neither rushed to tell me their secrets. I say *secrets*, because this was in an earlier era, before social media and the rush people now feel to expose every detail of their lives as a means of validating themselves to the world.

Back then, both women were still processing how they felt about this brief moment in time when they shared a moment with someone of Jim's stature. My sense was that they were each conflicted by who they were earlier in their lives. Neither was sure how their pasts jibed with who they felt they had become, like an upstanding adult who did something reckless as a teen and buried the secret in some deep recess.

Yet I had earned their trust by listening. Each of the conversations happened the same way, over a couple beers—not a Morrison-esque bacchanalia. Just friends chatting. Looking back, I think they believed that talking about it would release some of the pressure.

What I learned—decades before this book was formulated—fit with the view of Morrison that has since emerged and that I emphasize in these pages: he was a full person, containing a spectrum of complexities, just like most people. He wasn't just one thing—not the Lizard King, the drunk rock star, the poet, or the bandmate. He was all of them at the same time.

One of the women went on a date with Jim when he was in college at Florida State University. He was just a kid, but, in hindsight, only a handful of years removed from that young man walking the beach in Santa Monica. The Jim she knew was a kind person, funny and, as she described him, someone we would think of as a Southern gentleman. Their date, like most people experienced in the early Sixties, was innocent and fun.

Her memory was vivid, but it seemed she didn't want me (or anyone else who knew) to think she was bragging or attempting to make too much of a rather harmless college date. Just like Morrison, she later went to California and lived a hippie lifestyle. I don't remember if she was even a Doors fan in those ensuing years, but it seemed that she was troubled reconciling the Jim she knew with the public persona the world later knew.

The second woman met Jim in what I now realize must have been the Whisky days or in the interim between those gigs and "Light My Fire" becoming a hit. The woman described herself as young, pretty, and blonde, hippie-ish, but looking for a foothold in the world. She said that she went on a date with Jim but was sheepish about whether it was something formal or that they had met at a party or something similar.

Her memory of the night was interwoven with impressions of LA and the era, like a flower-child stereotype come to life. Her date with Jim, though, wasn't great, and it seemed she was almost embarrassed by that confession. Her primary memories of the night were that Morrison was drunk and pretentious, the budding rock star bragging or showing off. The vibe I got was that she felt ashamed—not only then, but in telling me the story decades later. As if she didn't live up to some internal measure that caused Jim to act that way. It seemed her unease was tangled up with the thought that she might have done something for him, rescued Morrison from himself—a desire to go back in the past and change the future for the better. Perhaps she carried guilt from the era and displaced it to this one night, as if she could recraft her life if she just would have acted in a different way. A moment in time that she still carried.

There are fewer and fewer people in the world today who knew Jim, let alone spent time with him, if only for a moment. Each of these women depicted him as one might assume based on a timeline of his life, yet these snapshots are revealing in what they tell us and also don't reveal. What intrigues me is that both of them met Morrison before he was a celebrity. They weren't asking something of him or expecting that he could provide anything.

There are others who knew him at the same time who would paint a completely different portrait. The aggregate, though, is key: Jim was a person living in the moment with a complex system of thinking about himself, his environment, and the people he engaged with. He was not bound to become the Lizard King, nor could he have predicted that outcome, just like these two women experienced him based on their interactions. In their cases, however, what they lived melded with what they would later learn, and perhaps continue to understand about him because he became iconic.

In researching this book, many Morrisons emerged. Yet, in themselves, these are also merely glimpses in time:

The Searcher: Always exploring for questions and answers, probing situations and people, trying to find the story, the truth. Using acid and alcohol to expand his perspectives.

The Artist: Notating his life and emotions, using himself and his environment as a canvas to create. Begging people to live in the moment rather than enslave themselves to society's expectations or mind-numbing tools, like television.

The Battler: Standing up to authority, whether it was his parents, teachers, or the police. The person willing to confront ideas, like making a senior thesis film that demonstrated the limitation of film-making. Creating and destroying personas as he evolved.

Mark Duffett, a music scholar and historian, sees "existentialism and nihilism" as central to Morrison and the band's sound. He links Jim's Paris death to this notion, calling him "a lost soul." What emerged from the music at its peak was what Duffett hears as "almost a kind of proto-postpunk band." Mixing Jim in with the punk movement—nihilism, rage, leather-clad—is a fascinating perspective on how the Doors sounded versus their peers. Yet they also came across like the underground college radio bands of the late Eighties, a precursor to REM or Echo and the Bunnymen, the latter of whom collaborated with Manzarek on a cover of "People Are Strange."

Bringing the real Jim full circle, in 2022 I spoke with Robert Josefsberg about the singer he had defended in Miami. He said Morrison was "electrifying"—you could feel the magnetism radiate from the young man—but at the same time "kind" and "a nice, decent human being with a sense of humor and sense of reality."

Toward the end of our conversation, however, Josefsberg grew reflective. He admitted, "I feel badly that after the trial I didn't stay in touch with Jim. I wish I would have called him and talked to him about sobriety, as one human being to another."

As I listened to the emotion in Bob's voice, I thought of the women who told me about their brief time with Jim. All three shared a common feeling: *I might have prevented what happened. I feel badly about that.*

"I liked him, I liked him very much," Josefsberg said. In that melancholy sentence, knowing that a young man died much too early, he captured what we share when we think about Jim Morrison.

Jim Morrison trained himself to sing. "You can hear him going on instinct," explained Elizabeth Bougerol, lead singer of the jazz band the Hot Sardines. "His use of growls, croaks, and so on, shows the kind of looseness and trust in the instrument that professionally trained singers sometimes shy away from for fear of damaging their vocal chords." His bandmates all remarked at one time or another about his "thin" voice at the beginning, while he matured into the vocalist he would later become.

Robby saw Morrison's vocal transformation up close. He compared the early Jim to the later Lizard King persona: "He wrote great lyrics, but he wasn't yet a crooning, leather-clad sex god. All I saw was a shaky-voiced, corduroy-clad introvert."

Quickly, though, Jim learned to let loose. He developed self-confidence and it powered his vocals. Ron Alan, a fellow musician who had played at London Fog before the Doors and became close friends with Jim, said, "He was good, he went for it. . . . You didn't look at him and say, 'There's a guy that's doubting his abilities.' I mean he was just doing it."

Morrison's idols were the great crooners who were popular when he was growing up in the 1950s. He used them as role models. When an interviewer asked about his influences and compared him to Elvis, Jim said "I'm not a new Elvis, though he's my second favorite singer—Frank Sinatra is first." Interestingly, he reportedly upset Sinatra by aping his vocal style on "Light My Fire." Sinatra was especially sensitive to the growing influence of rock and roll, and whether he meant it when he allegedly said he wanted to send someone to deal with Morrison, he wasn't pleased.

"The Sinatra influence is palpable," Bougerol explained. As a self-trained vocalist and music history aficionado, she can hear how Morrison picked up on the style of his favorite singer (buttressing Sinatra's claim about "Light My Fire"):

Once Sinatra joined Tommy Dorsey's orchestra, he wanted to sing like Dorsey played trombone: Long notes, rounded tone, held phrases that put the story of the song first. He paid a lot of attention to breath control, learning how to emulate Dorsey's legato (bound together) trombone style with his voice. Sinatra snuck breaths to sing longer and fuller phrases. You can hear Morrison using breath, holding notes, which really sets him apart from the more "conversational" singers who dominated the airwaves at the time—people like McCartney and Dylan, who sort of talk-sang, tossing off the lyrics, rarely holding notes. You could also say there's some Elvis in there in the rounded, breathy tones too.

We can view Morrison as a descendent of Presley in both the way he sang and the impact he had on audiences. Rock music historian Greil Marcus claimed that Jim had an "Elvis obsession." But he also "loved Bob Dylan," according to Morrison's sister Anne. "When Jim started getting records in high school, the first one I remember was *Freewheelin'* by Bob Dylan."

Bougerol's bandmate Evan Palazzo connects Morrison's "dynamic range of effects that seem to all come out of his natural personality. So he could do that kind of gritty singing and then he can also be sweet, and beautiful notes come out of him, somber and soft."

The connection between Morrison and Dylan is more subtle but shows itself in the way Jim used imagery and concepts to write lyrics. They were both influenced by the poets who dominated the 1950s and continued to inspire in the 1960s. "Morrison's lyrics feel like beat poetry, like Kerouac set to music," Bougerol explained. "A Morrison song feels less like a beginning-middle-and-end story and more of a sketch or an idea that he turns over to you, to flesh out and fill in those spaces in between."

"I really want to develop my singing. You know, I love the blues . . . I would like to get into that feeling and sing some old standards like 'St. James Infirmary.'"

—Jim Morrison

The biggest gulf between people's expectation of the Lizard King and the authentic Jim underneath the legend is in his nature. People who knew him consistently speak of him from this vantage point. "In Jim Morrison, I found to my surprise, a beautiful human being who has been a victim of sensational publicity and harassment by silly journalists," said writer Michael Cuscuna. Morrison "seems trapped in the routine of success, with a public image to live up to, while his best musical and cinematic talents and ambitions remain stifled and/or untapped."

According to Robby, Jim was a different person, particularly before the band had number one hits and gold albums. "He had a gentle nature when he wasn't screaming at drug dealers or getting in bar fights or nuking record deals," the guitarist remembered.

If Krieger ever had doubts about Jim, he could look to his own mother's impression. She found him pleasant, almost like a charming gentleman from an earlier age. A skeptic might wonder how much of Morrison's ability to win over women came from his budding charisma and possibly a need to find a mother figure, but the idea that Jim was an old-school, gentle charmer is one of the things people frequently remember about him.

One of Morrison's closest friends was filmmaker Frank Lisciandro, who saw through the myth. "He was gentle, compassionate, highly intelligent, and articulate. He cared about his poetry more than anything else—he only went into music as a way of incorporating his poetry."

Morrison's sensitivity and attraction to art were at odds with his drive toward self-destruction. Writer Tony Magistrale explained: "Morrison's personal demons drew him to the edge of the abyss and pushed him over into it. But until that point, a persistent faith in the transcendent powers of poetry and music helped to insulate him from that despair."

Ray Manzarek said that Jim's "tragic flaw" was to routinely attempt to "add more euphoria to his euphoria."

Jim's relationship with Pam—fraught with the unknowable intimacies only couples understand—looked like a lit bomb from the outside. Stories of their battles are legion and leave us troubled. Jim provoked her and Pam punched back—literally. Patricia Butler, who has studied their relationship more than any other historian or critic, concluded: "This tiny, sweet, angelic morsel who loved him, supported him, played with him, respected his art, and when provoked, wouldn't hesitate to haul off and punch him in the face."

Mirandi Babitz was a friend of Jim and Pam's. She and her husband Clem lived with them for a short time on the fabled "Love Street." She told Butler: "I never really felt comfortable around Jim. I thought he was weird; he was like black." However, she explained, that was part of the attraction between him and his soulmate. "I think Pam liked that, liked that sharp edge."

Jac Holzman saw similar battles, calling their union "a prickly relationship; a push-pull relationship." He and others who spent time with the couple watched as they attempted to one-up each other constantly.

"I think of myself . . .[as an] intelligent, sensitive human being with the soul of a clown that always forces me to blow it at the most important moments."

—Jim Morrison

We can't attempt to understand Jim without looking at his challenges with drugs and alcohol. The record of his drug use is cloudy and based primarily on the memories of those who knew him. Some claim he was sober for long periods or could at least be sober when necessary. For example, Michael McClure and Robert Josefsberg remember him abstaining when he needed to, but McClure also mentioned times when Jim did excessive amounts of cocaine. That said, there's little doubt he was in the process of drinking himself to death and that drugs played a role in his early demise.

"The positive side of Jim's excessiveness—his impulse to have everything and have it now!—channeled his angst into creativity," John explained. "The negative side of it, of course, would eventually surface as substance abuse." Krieger saw the transition from acid to booze as a way for Morrison "to balance himself out," since enormous amounts of LSD would eventually sizzle the brain.

The type and quantity of the drugs Jim took is a complicating factor and a point of debate, especially since he had an aversion to needles. Numerous sources confirm his acid use before the Doors and during the band's early days. But his later use of cocaine and other snortable drugs is less clear. Sometimes eyewitnesses even contradict themselves. Babe Hill, one of Jim's closest friends, spoke about doing a great deal of cocaine with Morrison. However, Hill then said, "the man was definitely not into drugs . . . no kind of drugs on a regular basis."

What we do know is that Jim saw alcohol as his path to revelation. He said once: "Every sip is another chance. Another flashing chance at bliss." Morrison privileged booze over other intoxicants and seemed to think it was a safer one too. We get a bit inside his head when thinking through what he told a reporter about the Doors, "We're a pretty sedate group—no dopers or sex maniacs or anything like that." *Normal* to Jim included—perhaps centered on—alcohol.

A sense of how Morrison perceived booze's role in helping him reach a different part of reality is found in his poem "The Opening of the Trunk." The voyage he planned for his mind is akin to a trunk, full of everything a person has ever experienced or felt. He equated freedom to that moment the trunk opened and finding an "infinite universe . . . revealed." Yet, as Morrison believed, the pathway to the infinite is too much for the soul. The mind cannot comprehend its boundlessness. As a result, the deep thinker is left astounded and stunned. He hurtles back to reality and the search for humanity—real flesh, "teachers & friends"—objects and ideas the mind can comprehend.

While acid played a role in creating the concert in his mind in the summer of 1965, it might be worthwhile to consider alcohol almost an acid-lite for Morrison. "The only time I really open up is onstage," Jim told a reporter. "The mask of performing gives it to me, a place where I hide myself then I can reveal myself. . . . I take everything really personally. I don't feel I've really done a complete thing unless we've gotten everyone in the theater on kind of a common ground." Did he need to feel inebriated to magnify his power over audiences? Booze took him to a place that intensified his connection to others and the moment, keeping him in a version of reality that acid eliminated.

What Morrison wanted was to light up listeners with his words, whether lyrics or poetic ad-libs plunked down within a familiar tune. During the explosive shows, however, when the air felt like a cauldron and he worked the audience into a frenzy, he turned to whatever worked—challenging them, lacing his pleas with expletives, calling their belief systems (and their very humanity) into question.

Rather than fear the energy unleashed, Jim begged for chaos. Lurching toward the darkness, he gave Doors concerts an edge that no other band could match. You went to a show with an expectation of chaos. Depending on Morrison's mood—and prodigious alcohol intake leading up to the performance—fans were witness to the bedlam and could expend their fears, frustrations, and fury. The resulting frenzy exploded into thrown chairs, fistfights, injuries, and arrests. "Fuck the world!" fans screamed. They could have it all and they could have it in that moment, even if fleeting.

"People are afraid of themselves, of their own reality—their feelings, most of all. People talk about how great love is, but that's bullshit. Love hurts. Feelings are disturbing. People are taught that pain is evil and dangerous. How can they deal with love if they're afraid to feel?"

—Jim Morrison

Jim's dependency on alcohol cut a path of destruction through his life. Ultimately, he used booze as a way to override his senses and exaggerate what he hoped to say to the world. Robby remembered him picking fights by provoking bullies and others in power positions, then letting them wale on him, rarely defending himself. "Was it masochism? Manipulation? Pushing emotional limits? Symbolically striking back at his authoritarian father?" Krieger asked. "I used to chalk it up to drunken stupidity—which it was—but now I recognize it as calculated drunken stupidity."

"The rock-and-roll lifestyle allowed the music industry to really chew up all these amazing and talented people . . . the list of casualties is in some ways astonishing and mind numbing," explains scholar Jesse Kavadlo. He likens the relationship to a kind of contract or "the narrative of rock music." In exchange for fame, money, and music immortality, the performer must be destroyed. "The excess and decadence can really only go in two directions, either death or burning out in obscurity."

Even more troubling, however, was when Jim's drunkenness hurt others—physical confrontations with Pam, asking women he had hooked up with to get abortions, destroying property via auto accidents or drunken escapades, and other excesses. "Liquor was always the catalyst," Robby contended. "Jim wouldn't even think of saying or doing something to start a fight when he was sober. He was always a perfect gentleman, even to cops."

~🦎~

"I'm so sick of everything. People keep thinking of me as a rock-and-roll star and I don't want anything to do with it. I can't stand it anymore. I'd be so glad if people didn't recognize me . . . who do they think Jim Morrison is, anyway?"
—Jim Morrison

"People see me all the time and they just can't remember how to act. Their minds are filled with big ideas, images, and distorted facts."
—Bob Dylan

~🦎~

Rock history is filled with artists who flamed out.

It's reasonable to think Jim knew this. About the deaths of Janis Joplin and Jimi Hendrix he said to a reporter: "[That] great creative burst is hard to maintain." Although Morrison seemed fascinated with the idea of death, his words and actions demonstrated that he didn't have a death wish. In his last phone call with John, he said he would be back to make new music. Earlier, when a journalist asked him how he would like to die, he replied in his usual soft drawl, "I hope at age one hundred twenty with a sense of humor and a nice comfortable bed. I wouldn't want anyone around. I just want to quietly drift off."

AFTERWORD
Jim Morrison in the Twenty-First Century

What can a singer dead for more than five decades tell us about twenty-first-century America? Well, if we're searching for insight from the life and enduring legend of Jim Morrison, the answer is contained in an unending string of impulses that combine to create the contemporary world.

Morrison matters today because we can use his brief life and long afterlife to examine the issues and topics that still bedevil modern society. From women's rights to our thinking about war and freedom, Morrison's vantage offers context. He also helps us understand philosophical questions about history, nostalgia, fame, and celebrity as an industry.

Looking at Morrison's life has another critical component—it demonstrates how our thinking transforms over time. The most straightforward example is how he was venerated in the 1980s by a generation who viewed him as the ultimate party animal. Following his lead, Gen Xers and others could give the middle finger to people in roles of authority while reveling in his booze-filled, hedonistic lifestyle.

While this perspective may always be a part of Morrison's legacy based on how young people choose to exert their freedoms, examining his life from today's viewpoint reveals a young man struggling with addiction and desperately in need of help. From Jim's life, we can learn much about addiction, recovery, and treatment in hopes of saving lives.

While generations of observers have filled Morrison with any number of meanings, near the end of his own life, he realized that he was on a search for something more. Even though many people would have traded their lifestyles for his in an instant, he hoped for a deeper purpose:

> I'm not denying that I've had a good time these last three or four years . . . met a lot of interesting people and seen a lot of things in a short space of time. . . . I can't say that I regret it, but if I had it to do over again, I would have gone more for the quiet, undemonstrative little artist plodding away in his own garden trip.

On a Sunday afternoon in February 1969, Jim Morrison went into a recording studio with engineer John Haeny to demo some of his poems before signing a contract with Elektra to do a full album. He had his notebooks with him, arranged in a specific order. His life was fairly incoherent at that time, but not when it came to his poetry. Morrison knew what he wanted to say and approached the project with determination.

After several attempts to get the sound correct, with Haeny fiddling with the knobs and controls, Jim launched into the tale of "soft mad children" who venture out into the night. Rather than the night being frightening or scary, the narrator portrayed it as containing limitless opportunities. The watcher lurked over the scene as naked couples "race" through the sand in solitude, completely to themselves. They laughed in the moonlight, laughing like only the young and innocent could. The gods called on them to frolic, sing, and dance. Reckless abandon, not unlike the Summer of Love as it has been remembered across time.

In a different scene, the innocents found themselves transported to mountainsides and forests on a dark "moonshine night" surrounded by thick trees. Still, they danced on. Yet as the joy filled the night sky, whether beach, lake, or milky moon, there was danger afoot.

A stolen knife and watching eyes portended the appearance of a sinister bird who preyed on the soul of the young poet, not taking him away but carrying dread and the silent souls of dead Native Americans, who had been killed anonymously in a senseless accident. Their broken bodies were thrown across an American highway, shoved further from their mystical heritage like broken Coke bottles, hollowed-out tires, and discarded fast-food wrappers that littered the roadway.

Throughout these verses and like so many that follow, the listener hears Morrison playing the role of interested observer, a kind of shaman. His words deliver a message asking that we focus on the timeless spirituality of dancing and joy, rather than the destructive consequences of the materialistic world. A couple's playful laughter stands in stark contrast to the death that pollutes a young child's delicate mind.

These same Native Americans would find themselves immortalized later that year in the song "Peace Frog" on the album *Morrison Hotel*. More than just a couple of spoken-word lines within a blues-infused rock tune, the interlude signaled that the forces of materialism had indeed emerged victorious. Their senseless deaths were caught up in a sea of chaos and blood. The singer felt helpless as the blood followed him wherever he looked or journeyed across time.

"Peace Frog" is a complex song in the guise of a rock tune. Though Morrison didn't expound on its meaning, the blood that flows so deep though the cities and countryside symbolized abortion ("runs red down the legs of a city" provides overt evidence). This topic had specific meaning for Jim, since several women he impregnated ultimately terminated—allegedly including Patricia Kennealy, who engaged in a pagan marriage ritual with him and considered herself his wife. (There are critics who question whether Kennealy was ever pregnant or if the baby was Morrison's.)

Given the Supreme Court overturning *Roe v. Wade*, women's rights to abortion have been curtailed, which threatens to put many in danger as they search for alternatives depending on the state they live in or healthcare they might access. Connecting Morrison to abortion might make some fans uneasy, but it is a topic that had meaning for him on several levels.

"I see myself as a huge fiery comet, a shooting star. Everyone stops, points up and gasps 'Oh, look at that!' Then whoosh, and I'm gone . . . and they'll never see anything like it ever again . . . and they won't be able to forget me—ever."

—Jim Morrison

If we collectively learned anything during the Covid pandemic, it is that we have a strange, complex, and enduring relationship with alcohol. In the days before a vaccine, as the world seemed to be crumbling down around us, all over America and across the globe, people found sanctuary in the bottle. It's not as if people hadn't always consumed booze, but almost overnight they fought off tragedy with YouTube mixologists, alcohol deliveries, and Zoom happy hours.

Here Jim's demise is instructive—you can't separate the person from the alcoholic. Drinking fueled Morrison in ways that most people only experience in hazy, day-after glimpses. He was careening down a dark highway with the lights off and his hands barely touching the wheel. But he was in control of the drinking—at least for a while. He knew the consequences, admitting publicly that he enjoyed what alcohol did to him, particularly versus smoking weed.

Like most drunks, the singer gradually lost control. At the end, there are reports of him pissing himself and passing out in bushes. No one likes to picture the Lizard King knock-down drunk and incontinent, but for those who have seen the downward slide of alcoholics, it is predictable.

"Jim rarely remembered his drunken fits, leaving the rest of us to pick up the pieces," Robby Krieger remembered. "His apologies were so simple, and yet so hypnotic. I still don't know how he got us to forgive him for half the stuff he did. There was something about his sober nature that made you feel bad about holding a grudge." This is another familiar scene for people who have dealt with alcoholics, especially highly charismatic ones like Morrison.

The peace, love, and happiness vibe of the Sixties halted when drunk Jim turned into the evil "Jimbo," the band's name for the other Morrison who came out like a scotch-fueled Jekyll and Hyde. His bandmates couldn't control Jimbo. Adding to the mess, he surrounded himself with a revolving cast of sycophants and hangers-on that turned his blackout stupors worse.

The guitarist called the band's reaction to Jimbo the "first shared act of burying our heads in the sand when it came to the erratic behavior of Jim Morrison." The more successful the Doors became, the more erratic Jim got. The situation deteriorated to the point that they just tried to keep him "as sober as possible on show nights." Yet the many extant recordings of Doors concerts reveal how futile that effort was.

Krieger learned that no amount of needling the singer worked, nor did "nagging" or "arguing." Morrison could not be intimidated into curtailing his intake. Robby, the junior member of the group in terms of age, wasn't going to impose his will on him, particularly because they had a kind of big brother–little brother relationship.

A reader today might scream, *Where's the intervention?* To imagine that outcome, however, would be to take the Sixties out of context. Over and over again since the era, Ray, Robby, and John consistently pointed to the laidback nature of the decade. No one came at drinkers or drug users too aggressively—everyone was drunk or stoned—no judgment.

In the Sixties, the stigma against discussing alcoholism was rampant. Many physicians helped people cover up the disease—because they weren't sure how to help or didn't want to get involved. An early effort at changing this state of affairs took place in 1969 when Senator Harold E. Hughes, a Democrat from Iowa, distinguished himself by leading a nationwide education effort to alert people to the dangers of alcoholism.

Hughes, who'd had a personal battle with alcohol, championed the cause by holding public hearings on alcoholism and narcotics. At the subsequent subcommittee hearings, experts estimated that about five to six million Americans were then alcoholics (a figure thought to be underestimated). Although state and federal government agencies collected about eight billion dollars on sales of alcohol, only four million was spent on fighting the scourge.

In a congressional research report, physician John L. Norris explained:

> We in medicine are grossly unprepared, technically and philosophically [to treat alcoholism], for we share the ambivalence and active disinterest of the rest of society. . . . We have little idea how much of a present problem is caused by alcohol itself, nor do we have as yet any physical sign or psychological finding which distinguishes those who can drink safely from those who cannot.

Carl Erik Fisher, an addiction psychiatrist who teaches at Columbia University, places the struggle in context, explaining, "For years, psychiatry labored under the idea that mental disorders were categorical, fixed entities—things people got—but today there is a rising recognition that all mental disorders seem to exist on a continuum." The barriers have started to fall, but the complete eradication of the stigma has not been achieved.

According to psychotherapist Jeannine Vegh, there is still a long way to go. "I think that our society still shuns people living with addictions. We see it as a weakness that needs to be overcome." In Jim's specific case, she explains, "An addict is someone with mental-health problems. They are self-medicating. Getting clean and sober is a difficult task for the person who wants to avoid pain and stay in denial."

While we continue to uncover new thinking about addiction and other brain-related topics, Morrison's experience as a person addicted to alcohol compels us to reconsider his life, from the outlandish behavior to his early death.

What we do not get from Morrison—as a person with a full range of human complexities—is a single perspective or fixed point on how to interpret him or his era. He is part of a larger puzzle for understanding the Sixties and early Seventies. What I argue, along with other historians, is that history is the craft of presenting information based on viewpoints, analysis, documentation, and other points of reference, but not what actually happened. Even if you were beside Jim as he lived his life, it would not be history but rather your interpretation of that time frame from your own perspective. Historians create the framework.

This is important in examining and piecing together a contentious era like the Sixties. We are attempting to shine light into the dark night that brings together the lived experiences and lifetimes of people who valued the time for different reasons. For example, I contend that it is impossible to comprehend the Sixties without layering in Vietnam, whether economic, political, or cultural. However, I've interviewed people who have never mentioned the war or its consequences on their lives. It is not as if these individuals lived in an alternate reality; it's just that they found a way to circumvent the topic in a way that makes sense to them in their recollections.

Even when examining the parts of the Sixties that seemed to flow logically into the next, for example, as if the self-help and meditation of the 1970s had to be the outcome of the free-love and activist 1960s, we understand this equation is never the straight line it might appear to be on paper, film, or video. In fact, when it does seem like a direct path, it's most likely that someone has created that narrative.

For literary critic Morris Dickstein, who grew up in the 1960s, a multitude of influences melded to create the era's foundation: "The cold war, the bomb, the draft, and the Vietnam War gave young people a premature look at the dark side of our national life, at the same time that it galvanized many older people already jaded in their pessimism." The role the Doors played in exposing the dark side and bringing it to the mainstream is significant.

The depth of Morrison's life called for writing this book. Few cultural icons have had a more lasting impact. But, as I have shown, the importance of the Doors includes the group too. It wasn't strictly the Jim Morrison show, although his myth is of course a big factor in the band's enduring fame.

This book is a reassessment of a significant era in American history and an example of how we might gain from that exercise. According to David Strutton and David G. Taylor: "The examination of history allows one to acquire experience by proxy; that is, learning from the harsh or redemptive experiences of others. . . . Mythology is less reliable than history as narrative of actual experience; yet it may hold more power than history."

By revisiting Morrison, the Doors, and the death days of the Sixties, we give the era meaning as it existed in its day and at the same time create a tool to use to navigate our lives and the future. For example, Vietnam has become synonymous with America's intervention in overseas wars, particularly against enemies that appear doomed on paper. The wars in the Middle East over the last several decades have been examined via the Vietnam lens, but the comparison sadly did not lead to a different outcome. In this case—and concerning future warfare—we might ask ourselves the reasonable question: Where were the protesters who played such a pivotal role in illuminating what was happening in Southeast Asia in the Sixties and Seventies? For that matter, why were the journalists in the Middle East "embedded" rather than emboldened like their media forbearers? Perhaps the most significant difference was the draft, but the real emphasis is that reevaluating the decades gives a measure of what is happening today—and offers a potential lens for anticipating the future.

Reevaluating and analyzing the Sixties helps us see the era without giving undue weight to nostalgia. Just like the critically-acclaimed television show *Mad Men*, a truthful depiction built on sound judgment will help modern audiences better assess the period.

Many observers have begun to appraise the Baby Boomers and the negative effect they've had on American life as the generation continues to exert its power societally. Observing how the Boomers acted as young people and then changed over time is another example of how the cross-examination role modeled in this book helps us chart a future course. Bruce Cannon Gibney sees the generation displaying "sociopath" tendencies that have hurt the nation, or at least prevented it from realizing its potential. "America suffers from its present predicament because a large group of small-minded people chose the leaders and actions that led to our present degraded state," he explains. Rather than keep the nation on a better path, the Boomers sold out their youthful idealism in exchange for self-interest.

Matt Weiner, the creator of *Mad Men*, echoes this sentiment, which he experienced as a child. What he saw, he told a reporter, was "the world being run by a bunch of hypocrites . . . repressive, selfish, racist, moneygrubbing."

At the same time, though, much of popular culture is dedicated to nostalgia. The concept is central to mass communication and the way people think. The list of mass media that use nostalgia as a primary theme is endless, since many creative pieces hinge on looking back, whether with pride, agony, anxiety, or joy. Every era is filled with nostalgia-based programming.

For example, entire television networks have been built around reruns. As a result, even mediocre shows like *The Brady Bunch* and *Three's Company* have aired for decades and exuded undue influence over viewers. Films have been similar, such as the desire to watch *It's a Wonderful Life* every holiday season or the many Rankin/Bass stop-motion Claymation specials. Even though these programs have been viewed dozens or hundreds of times, there is still a yearning that plops down viewers in front of them once again, particularly if it involves passing the shows onto children who represent the next generation of nostalgia consumers.

Mad Men brought the disconnect between the generations to life for a new age. Two characters argued about a client presentation, with the hippie ultimately railing that his older colleague has his "fascist boot on my neck." The agency partner then pointed out the hypocrisy of the counterculture movement, calling him one of the "hippies who cash checks from Dow Chemical and General Motors."

We all need tools to examine society's larger questions, but Morrison's life can also help us understand each other on a more intimate level. How did Jim view himself in the world?

One of the most striking aspects of Jim's life versus the legend that grew after he died is the gap between what people thought of the public person versus the more private individual. After his death, the mythmaking and apocryphal aspects of his life seemed to eclipse who he really was.

For example, journalist Michael Cuscuna said, "The antithesis of his extroverted stage personality, the private Morrison speaks slowly and quietly with little evident emotion, reflectively collecting his thoughts before he talks. No ego, no pretensions." For writer Dylan Jones, Jim stood as "the first rock 'n' roll method actor" and "an intellectual in a snakeskin suit." Ultimately, hinting at the singer's true nature, he saw "a man who, when he revealed himself, was often to be found simply acting out his own fantasies."

Jim embraced this notion of self-creation and wore different masks publicly and privately. In 1968, Morrison admitted that his image as the Lizard King was "all done tongue-in-cheek." He explained, "It's not to be taken seriously. It's like if you play the villain in a Western that doesn't mean that's you." But the singer cautioned, "I don't think people realize that." Were these really different masks for Morrison, or did the true Jim get lost (or stuck) in the alcoholic stupor?

Before the band hit the big time, there were some musicians and hippies in Los Angeles who saw Jim as little more than a poseur, as someone who wanted to become part of the scene and yearned for attention and approval. They saw him not as a poet but as just another lost angel longing for fame and fortune in the City of Lights.

A foundational aspect of human life is the need to create meaning. People engage in this activity from birth, investigating and examining the world in relation to other people and things around them. This type of exploration is called semiotics, which in plain terms means asking what something means in relation to ourselves and others. From this vantage point, Morrison's public persona was cast in symbolic terms, like how a celebrity/star acted and what they could get away with versus noncelebrities. When he yelled out, "I am the Lizard King . . . I can do anything!" it seemed he believed it—at least the version of Jim who had assumed that symbolic role.

People use symbols, then, to adapt to a complex world that contains an enormous amount of abstraction. Krieger pinned Morrison's worldview on his antiauthority nature. "You couldn't tell Jim Morrison what to do. And if you tried he would make you regret it," the guitarist recalled. "He was forever rebelling against his Navy officer father. Anyone who attempted to step into a role of authority over him became the target of his unresolved rage." What he learned to lash out at was not his powerful father but those in authority who attempted to control him.

Psychotherapist Vegh saw the lasting effects of growing up in a military family. "Jim suffered from a crisis in his mind. His words seem destined for a prophet, but, instead, he succumbed to drink and drugs. I assumed that he had been exposed to some form of family trauma." She believes it may have been that his parents preferred "dressing down" to other forms of punishment. "When a child is berated and humiliated in front of others, it takes a toll on them spiritually, physically, and mentally." The turmoil from this kind of upbringing is a clear factor in Jim basically disowning his parents even before he became famous. When his father told him that joining a band was stupid, he never forgave him and never spoke to him again.

Morrison, by studying film, literature, and sociology, understood more deeply and theoretically what his contemporaries like Jagger, McCartney, Lennon, and Joplin knew—fame served as one of many disguises he had to wear as a rock star. For Jim, there was the hyperindividual aspect of fronting a band and presenting himself to an audience and then there was the other piece of it, the communal vibe from the collective experience. That high from being on stage—the rush of emotion, the intensity, the energy—was likely another form of addiction for him.

When in his rock-star guise, Jim could also turn into the hideous performer, especially when drunk. If Morrison didn't feel or perceive what he wanted from the audience, he turned against them, essentially doing what he did in one-on-one relationships: goad and aggressively provoke a reaction—any reaction. "I don't feel I've really done a complete thing unless we've gotten everyone in the theater on kind of a common ground," he said. "Sometimes I just stop the song and just let out a long silence, let out all the latent hostilities and uneasiness and tensions before we get everyone together."

Yet whether the show went well frequently depended on the other principal ingredient—alcohol. The booze distorted his perceptions, which the singer believed helped him reach new horizons, but the mixed-up sensitivities of an alcohol-addled mind washed out of him in ways that neither he nor the band completely understood. Misperception led to the attempted riot and arrest in New Haven and the beginning-of-the-end Miami incident.

Morrison realized and manipulated the power he possessed as *rock star* and purposely baited the crowd in ways that were new to them. A person going to a concert has expectations and understands (roughly) how they should act as a part of the community. The Doors, however, constantly messed with that pact because it titillated Jim's worldview and allowed him to see both his *true* self and his growing authority after a lifetime of poking at the figures and institutions of power in his life. Morrison told a reporter: "I like to see how long they can stand it, and just when they're about to crack, I let 'em go."

Once questioned about what might happen to him if the crowd turned, even threatening his own safety, Jim responded in typical narcissistic fashion, claiming, "I always know exactly when to do it." Rather than fear them or what they might do to him, he craved control over the masses. "That excites people. . . . They get frightened, and fear is very exciting. People like to get scared." Intensifying his controversial comments, he used sex as an analogy: "It's exactly like the moment before you have an orgasm. Everybody wants that. It's a peaking experience." The domination over the crowd and its collective retort fascinated and mesmerized Morrison. He could directly influence their experience or lead the band into a frenzy—with Ray and Robby urging the emotional response while John pounded out a driving beat.

Examining Bob Dylan's career, you can see similar uses of the mask metaphor as a way to make sense of complexity and abstraction. In the early 1970s, Dylan faced a period of agitation as he coped with the decline of his marriage to his wife Sara. Looking back on the period, he spoke about the many sides of himself that existed and kind of threw him off-kilter. Dylan explained: "I was constantly being intermingled with myself, and all the different selves that were in there, until this one left, then that one left, and I finally got down to the one that I was familiar with."

To cope with fame, Dylan constantly created new personas and masks. He could alternatively exist as a singer, writer, musician, revolutionary, poet, degenerate, or any of the other labels that might be thrust at him. Dylan even spoke about himself in the third person to underscore the difference between him and the character named "Bob Dylan."

Obviously, while there is ultimately a person there—waking each day, eating, working, daydreaming, bathing—there is another aspect of Dylan that defies simple definition. Dylan, a member of an elite category of iconic figures, exists outside his physical form and represents numerous meanings that give people a tool to interpret the world around them. As a result, the artist isn't only a member of society but a set of interpretations and symbols that help others generate meaning. As fans and onlookers, people are familiar with this trade-off. They accept it with each side gaining something in the exchange. A *regular* human being could *never* have handled the pressure of being called the spokesperson of a generation. Instead, Dylan used different personas to compartmentalize and make sense of it—until he snapped under the weight of drugs and booze and used a motorcycle accident in 1966 as an excuse to drop out. Some would call Dylan's breakdown a natural result of a burden too heavy to carry.

The difference between Dylan and Morrison is that the latter died before he had to confront these many roles. In death, these roles are assigned to Morrison by fans, critics, historians, and observers. Both icons might ask—if possible—that we define them by the songs they created or the lyrics they wrote, but the larger culture wants so much more. There is an image that must be created, managed, and maintained. Once someone becomes famous or iconic, they hold two identities—symbol and person.

Yet according to Evan Palazzo of the Hot Sardines, the power of the music is the real testament to the Doors. "Imagine if you were a concert buff in 1968, 1969, 1970, the bands you could see live, it was unparalleled. We don't have anything like that today," he explains. "But if they were a new band, the Doors would blow everyone out of the water—it would be seismic."

For today's listeners—no longer enslaved to vinyl, CD, or cassette because of the transformation to streaming music services—the Doors are just part of the classic-rock genre. For younger listeners, the band is on a playlist or "decontextualized as a fifty-year-old band," according to Jesse Kavadlo. "My college students don't experience music like we did pre-Internet. It's just playlist stuff. All the music is available instantly, so they relate to it differently."

It doesn't even really matter that Jim is dead. For so many people, his spirit is as real as a brick wall, the latest Doors release on Spotify, or a video on YouTube.

"I tell you this man, I tell you this . . . I don't know what's gonna happen, man, but I wanna have my kicks before the whole shithouse goes up in flames."

—Jim Morrison

My Doors Memoir

remember the exact moment I fell in love with Jim Morrison and the Doors.

The summer of 1986 I was seventeen. I lived with my aunt and her family in a beat-up trailer in a little collection of six or so of them near my hometown. Because she and my uncle worked pretty much around the clock, they needed help around the house. I needed to escape a less-than-satisfying living situation. One week they took their two little girls camping—probably their only vacation that summer and definitely unpaid from their jobs. I doubt they even had benefits. My grandmother had given me a couple bags of food and a little cash to, as she said, "make sure you don't starve."

My buddies—Chris, Mersh, and B.T.—had already taken the money over to the beer distributor in our little Western Pennsylvania college town, waiting to ambush an unsuspecting college student: "Will you buy us some beer, man? We'll give you the change." It always worked . . . and they rarely took the money, of course, since they had been in our shoes in the not-so-recent past.

Mersh, the fastest of the fast-talkers among our friends, persuaded the student to get us a keg, putting down a deposit and signing a fake name. I don't remember the exact cost, but the rotgut we drank back then was probably around twenty bucks, plus ten for the deposit. We had also each squirreled away a motley crew of liberated beers, half-empty bottles of whiskey, and pilfered vodkas from various family members, refrigerators out in the garage, and older siblings.

We had a heck of a party that first night, just the four of us and a handful of close friends. Nothing major—sedate and full of music, singing, and happiness about being alive and alone. The next morning, with the sun just cresting the horizon, I woke up on a couch in the screened-in porch to a familiar sound—"Roadhouse Blues" by the Doors.

Sliding through the door, I saw B.T. standing over the keg—which had mysteriously moved from the outdoor fridge to now sit in an oversized barrel in the middle of the living room—just as Morrison exclaimed that he woke up to get himself a beer. In that moment, the sunlight glinting through the windows, feeling the majesty of not having any adults around, and seeing one of my best friends pour himself a beer at sunrise elated me. I fell in love with the Doors instantly after simply digging them for years.

Then (as now), Morrison personified the *idea* of revolt and standing up to authority, thus his appeal to young people—particularly men—has been in how one can live that experience within the limitations of ever-present authority. In the case of my friends in the 1980s, living a kind of quasi-*Footloose* existence in a tiny, conservative town, putting Jim's perceived hedonism on a pedestal allowed us to think we were rebels or radicals.

Constantly under pressure from teachers, coaches, and parents (Baby Boomers who were erratically in and out of the picture, wantonly asserting dominance and sometimes disappearing completely), we found dark gods in the Doors. We could imagine Morrison dying for our sins. He was brave where we were weak. Emulating him, we could be whoever we wanted, if only for a night in a drunken haze.

Our high school was odd—you had to choose sides on just about everything, including music heroes. As a result, you were peer-pressured into choosing between the Beatles and the Stones and the Doors or Led Zeppelin. No one slid between teams—one or the other! If anything personifies the 1980s more, there were actually knock-down, drag-out fist-fights over these selections. Even though I know this was a questionable position, I have to admit that I'm still not much of a Beatles fan—though certainly understand their significance—and, of course, I like Zeppelin, but in a qualified way.

More than thirty-five years later, however, I still love the Doors, even as that specific memory fades. I doubt B.T. would remember that morning or that still-cold draft he poured—I haven't talked to him since he high-tailed it out of PA in the early Nineties, though I hear from his sister that he's doing well out in the wilds of the Great American West. And I could write an entire book about the individual and collective lives of the people I introduced in this little story; how they unraveled and reassembled over the decades.

What still resonates, though, is that a bright, shining flash in a young life filled with heartache and true despair led all these years later to the book you're reading. There are countless people who have a connection to a band or performer, book, film, or television show that mysteriously changed them.

My love affair with the Doors and Jim Morrison has never ended and has instead plunged me deeper into an attempt to get at who he was and what their music has meant to an audience that must number in the hundreds of millions. I think a biographer or historian is often directed toward a topic. The eminent writer Jerome Charyn, one of the greatest authors this nation has ever produced, once told me: "All my books are really about me." *Roadhouse Blues* fits within Charyn's sentiment.

I want to understand Morrison and the Doors because I want to decipher my own life, as well as America writ large across the ages. Yet how do you put something as large and complex as America into words or even a single person? A writer can never really understand what is inside the mind of another person. Even if we spent a lifetime trying, we could never fully unravel their thoughts, no matter the level of deep conversation, analysis, and thinking that takes place. Even then, we only see the masks our subjects are willing to show or reveal.

My mental model of cultural history is that one takes context and influences from every aspect of life to create as full a portrait as possible of a topic, person, or thing. Picking apart the assumptions or legends of a life and then trying to add to the body of knowledge is a worthy—and frequently difficult—task that necessitates the synthesis of mountains of information. Yet there are always holes to fill in and that takes interrogation, inference, and examination. To paraphrase my mentor Phillip Sipiora: one does not need to find answers, the power is in the analysis.

The goal of *Roadhouse Blues* is straightforward—to examine how the Doors became the Doors, think through their lasting impact on American and global culture, and assess how we have traditionally thought about Jim Morrison versus how we might revise that thinking based on new ideas and interpretations.

For example, there are many laughable moments with Morrison—his life was decidedly *not* all doom and gloom or drugs and alcohol. Just about everyone who knew him and put their memories down in print said that he loved to laugh and had several corny (definitely not PC) one-liners at his disposal that cracked him up every time he repeated them.

What few have fully captured is the complexity of the individual life. Here's a guy whose intellectual curiosity is clearly relentless. He bats ideas around like a cat with a toy, but sometimes uses his wit to outthink and possibly even manipulate those around him. Morrison has an intense, and seemingly cemented, worldview. These principles guide him. Yet so does his growing alcohol dependency.

Look at the lyrics, the mammoth collection of poems, other writing he did, the interviews and appearances. These all are apart from the amazing music he and the Doors made—wholly unique to their era and today. No one else sounds like the Doors.

So Morrison lived as and became a creative force, but over time he regretted that it was in music and not writing. He attacked fame but came to realize the cost to his true nature. Then the arrests, the pressures, the dependency. Jim had a vision of what life could become and lived on a trajectory that led to an ignoble end.

What I do know for sure—because I've had this discussion with many, many people—is that my love for the Doors and the forever-young Jim Morrison is not unique, nor will it end soon.

Break on though . . . all right!

ACKNOWLEDGMENTS

As a cultural historian and biographer, I have racked up some debts in my pursuit in writing *Roadhouse Blues*. Thanks to Robert Josefsberg, Morrison's co-counsel during his Miami trial, for providing a vivid portrait of the singer during that traumatic time. Bob also read some pages and gave me his thumbs-up, particularly regarding one potentially sensitive assertion I've made. His support—for a guy writing a book who he didn't previously know—means so much. I also want to thank the two anonymous women who shared their thoughts about Jim and the details of their time with him. The list of people who knew Morrison personally grows smaller by the day. These firsthand accounts have enlivened *Roadhouse Blues* immeasurably.

Another goal was to examine aspects of the Doors history and Morrison's life through the lens of contemporary America to get a sense—if only to a small degree—of what it might have been like to be a member of the band or its singer. Related to this aspiration was the plan to speak to musicians, vocalists, therapists, and addiction specialists in an attempt to conceive two distinctly different questions. First, how did the Doors create their unique sound and stay so popular across these many decades? Second, how would our modern thinking about addiction, recovery, and other mental health topics expand our thoughts about Morrison?

I would like to thank Elizabeth Bougerol, the vocalist and co-band-leader of the great jazz band the Hot Sardines, for her insight on technique, jazz history, and stage presence. Evan Palazzo, pianist and co-bandleader of the Hot Sardines, gave me deep insight into Manzarek's style, how the Doors created their sound, and music history. I have been an admirer of Jesse Kavadlo's scholarship for more than a decade. He has written astutely about numerous topics, from Don DeLillo and *Fight Club* to Michael Chabon and contemporary popular culture. He is highly accomplished—and maybe the only person to do both of these things simultaneously—as professor of English and Humanities at Maryville University in St. Louis and guitarist for Top Gunz, a popular Eighties rock tribute band. My discussion with Jesse gave me deep insight into rock guitar, music culture, and how young people related to music. Ben Golder-Novick, the acclaimed saxophonist and instrumentalist, provided detailed analysis of musicianship, playing in front of large crowds, and more. I appreciate the writing and wisdom of Mark Duffett of the University of Chester (UK), who is a fantastic rock historian and thinker.

Psychotherapist Jeannine Vegh enabled me to understand Morrison on a deeper level. Her analysis of his poems and episodes from his life and background provided a rich illustration of ideas that formed to create and influence him. Chad Kingsbury, an accomplished teacher and researcher in addiction recovery, shared many ideas about how we might view Morrison today. Over the years, I've had many conversations about addiction recovery with my friend Chris Burtch that have transformed the way I conceive of dependency and renewal.

Roadhouse Blues would not have been possible without the support and friendship of Kyle Sarofeen at Hamilcar Publications. Our partnership led to *Roadhouse Blues*, because we believe in producing strong content and feel that it will find readers in the mixed-up, muddled-up world of 24/7 media saturation. Under Kyle's able guidance, Hamilcar has become one of the great publishing houses around. Shannon LeMay-Finn provided great copyediting and oversight. Brad Norr is a phenomenal designer! I treasure his work and am certain you have too.

This book is the culmination of a lifetime of reading, research, and thinking and discussing American culture. There is a brief essay on sources, so I won't take up space here discussing the mountain of information. Instead, let me thank several institutions that provided materials, including the Blue Ash branch of the Cincinnati & Hamilton County Public Library and its electronic resources, Stow-Munroe Falls Public Library, Lane Public Library, and the Cleveland Public Library system.

I don't know how historians ever lived without interlibrary loan and electronic records databases. I used OhioLINK extensively, Hoopla Digital, and OverDrive. To get a sense of the era and read the journalism of that day, Newspapers.com is invaluable. I appreciate Raychel Lean at ALM for sharing her published interview with Bob Josefsberg.

There are many friends who provided thoughtful support, discussion, or encouragement on this journey. I would like to thank several friends and scholars who helped me, including Arthur Asa Berger, who is simply one of the nation's great creative minds. Thank you to Carl Rollyson—in my mind the Dean of American Biography—who always says, "The answer to one biography is another biography." His work is inspirational and his encouragement is much appreciated.

I am constantly inspired to be a stronger writer and thinker by Jerome Charyn. He has had a profound impact on me. Thank you too to Jerome's wife Lenore Riegel for continued friendship and support. I am constantly buoyed by my mentor and friend Phillip Sipiora, whose influence is found on every page. As always, to the memory of the great historian Lawrence S. Kaplan.

My thinking about history, life, and friendship has been shaped and formed by Thomas Heinrich. He is more than a friend—a brother for life. Josh Schwartz is a trusted friend, advisor, and confidante. Thanks to my friends at the Diversity Movement, particularly Don Thompson and Jackie Ferguson. Brian Jay Jones is one of America's best writers and biographers, I am thankful for his encouragement.

I always write with the memory of my mother-in-law, Josette Hérupé Percival Valois, near. I would also like to extend my thanks to Michel and Lisa Valois, Carole and Laurent van Huffel, Matthew and Trang van Huffel, Benjamin van Huffel, and Nicholas van Huffel.

Finally, nothing is possible without the love and support a writer receives from their family. Thank you to Kassie and Sophia for all the love in the world! I learn so much from them, even though they probably don't realize it. They both think the "little girl" references in Doors lyrics are pretty creepy—their Gen Z minds hear those flashes totally different from their Gen X dad.

My wife Suzette is my research partner, co-writer, best friend, and my North Star. Thank you—my love—for everything. I love you!

A final word, if you will indulge me—the Doors have provided one of the most significant soundtracks of my life. *Immense joy* is not nearly enough to encapsulate what this music has meant to me. Of course, one eventually gravitates to Jim Morrison. That idol I put on a pedestal when I was a teenager is not the same person I consider now that those years are long, long gone. As an adult, with children older than I was when I fell in love with the Doors, I reflect on his young life and shake my head in disbelief—what a tragedy that he did not live to fulfill what could have been an even greater life.

SOURCES: AN ESSAY

A researcher could spend their life immersed in the Doors and Jim Morrison. Take, for example, roughly 126 million hits on a search for the band on Google. There are millions of videos of the Doors and Morrison on YouTube.

If you don't have decades to dedicate to the pursuit of Morrison and the Doors, here's a plan: start with primary research—the actual music. Jumping into the Doors rabbit hole begins with the music. Stream the albums in order and get a feel for how the Doors sound evolved. Mix in some YouTube videos of them playing so that the imagery and sound melds. The spectacle of concerts by the Doors is where all four bandmates came to life. Next, watch some interviews and then read the memoirs of Ray, Robby, and John. If at that point you're still on the chase, expand your listening to include other great bands of the Sixties and Seventies, which must include the Beatles, Bob Dylan, the Rolling Stones, Jimi Hendrix, Janis Joplin, the Grateful Dead, the Who, and on and on.

If you're a vinyl hunter (like me), good luck finding original Doors albums, unless you're lucky or plan to break the bank. I like to find things out in the wild, at antique malls or the like. You can cheat, however, and just go to eBay and have all six studio albums in your hands pretty fast.

The best alternative path to Doors enlightenment might be to watch a series of films and television shows to get a sense of the Sixties and early Seventies. *Mad Men* or *Forrest Gump* is going to be more visceral for most young people than reading a book about the era. Also check out *The Graduate* (1967) or *Easy Rider* (1969), which will provide lots of context and all the flavor of the age.

Another fruitful avenue would be to roll, baby, roll over to the *Woodstock* (1970) documentary or explore *Monterey Pop* (1968), which focuses on several of the era's biggest stars, such as Janis Joplin and Jimi Hendrix (who plays in both). In 2014, CNN ran a miniseries called *The Sixties*, which was produced and narrated by Tom Hanks. It is readily available and rerun on the news network fairly frequently. If you think the Sixties was like a box of chocolates, then the fun of the CNN series is its comprehensive view narrated by Forrest himself—though not in his distinctive Alabama accent. The real power, however, is in the archival footage and voices used to bring the decade to life. You won't be on a time-travel machine, but you'll hear the voices and see the people who were influencing and creating the decade.

I've already written about Oliver Stone's *The Doors* (1991), so the point is basically that Ray, Robby, and John didn't like it or think that it accurately reflected the Jim Morrison they knew so well. They all dug Val Kilmer's portrayal of Jim, however, as did many other Doors insiders, including several people who knew Morrison and were brought to tears.

The Doors is Hollywood history; its primary goal is entertainment. Once you've studied the era and read some of the books mentioned below, the composite characters and the outrageous picture of Morrison will jump out at you from the screen, but it's one perspective that should be considered. I would hazard a guess that most people currently get their views and ideas about Morrison and the Doors from the movie. When people talk to me about Morrison, it's frequently their views about Kilmer-as-Morrison, not the actual rock star.

Given the tens of thousands of books about the Flower Power era, the Vietnam War, Lyndon B. Johnson, Richard Nixon, Bob Dylan, and countless additional topics, you might think that there have been many, many books on the Doors. Think again!

All the members of the Doors—outside Morrison—have written memoirs, so that is the starting place for understanding the band. John was the first, publishing *Riders on the Storm: My Life with Jim Morrison and the Doors* in 1990—perfect timing since Stone's film was released the following year. Given Ray's unofficial titles as spokesperson for Jim's memory and band historian, it is surprising Ray waited most of a decade for his book, *Light My Fire: My Life with the Doors* (1998). After years of squabbling over how the band's name and licensing would be used, a series of big-money lawsuits led to internal battles pitting Ray and Robby against John, with Jim's estate taking one side or another. Densmore wrote about these fights in *The Doors Unhinged: Jim Morrison's Legacy Goes on Trial* (2013). In 2020, John published his memoir on creativity and creative inspiration, *The Seekers: Meetings with Remarkable Musicians (and Other Artists)*. The most recent—and long-awaited—memoir is Robby Krieger's *Set the Night on Fire: Living, Dying, and Playing Guitar with the Doors* (2021).

The books by Ray, Robby, and John are essential for examining the life and times of each band member, their significance as one of the great American rock bands, and their lives with and without Morrison. Each memoir is fun to read. Of the three, Ray's is written in exactly the voice you would expect of Manzarek—hippie slang, mystical lyricism, and full of hype, hype, hype. Given the most time to contemplate the meaning of his life fused with the band and iconography of the Doors, Robby's book struck me as the deepest and saddest, particularly given his post-Doors drug addiction.

As I discussed with Jesse Kavadlo, the remaining members of the band have spent the rest of their lives talking about those handful of years. As a result, they have kind of, from Jesse's perspective, been placed "in a bubble" along with Jim—forever young, forever reliving that era over and over again. Can you imagine the pressure of being forced to be the spokesperson for Jim and the Sixties for the rest of your life—no matter what you ever hoped to achieve or are doing currently?

No one is going to cry a river of tears for the remaining Doors or Jim's estate given the amount of money the band generated and continues to make, but these are still human beings with emotions, guilt, dreams, and aspirations. I'm sure none of them wanted their lives to end—in the eyes of the public—when the world found out that Jim had died.

The surviving members of the Doors collaborated with famed *Rolling Stone* editor Ben Fong-Torres on an illustrated history, *The Doors* (2006).

Lots of previously unpublished photos and info from Ray, Robby, and John give the book value. In this vein, I recommend John Rocco's *The Doors Companion* (1997), a collection of interviews, articles, and new essays on the enduring popularity of the band. The mix of older material with new scholarly-informed essays makes Rocco's book essential reading.

No matter what you or I thought of James Douglas Morrison as a human being, his aspiration was to write poetry. Therefore, approach Jim as a poet. Morrison self-published a couple books and by all accounts was proud of them. He hoped the reception would help him establish himself outside the band and let him pursue other creative avenues, which included scriptwriting and filmmaking, and maybe even acting.

In the last two weeks, I had one person randomly tell me that Morrison was "an awful poet," essentially writing "drivel." There is not much meat to that criticism, nor did they provide examples of what was so appalling. However, another person in that same time frame told me that Morrison would have had a future as a serious poet and cited Michael McClure's support as validation. Interestingly, McClure himself has been kind of lost to us versus where his reputation stood while he was while alive. In his era, the poet was a giant among the Beats, yet when most people think of that era, it is Allen Ginsberg, Jack Kerouac, and Lawrence Ferlinghetti who frequently come to mind. McClure's sponsorship and friendship may have helped Morrison climb that intellectual hurdle, though the power of celebrity may have proved a barrier.

In 2021, Morrison's estate brought out *The Collected Works of Jim Morrison: Poetry, Journals, Transcripts, and Lyrics*, edited by Frank Lisciandro. Of course, the book garnered intense media coverage and shot onto the *New York Times* Bestseller List. Clocking in at about six hundred pages, the collection includes songs, poetry, snippets of narrative work, and a film treatment. Interspersed within the text are photos of Jim's real loose-leaf notebook pages, his handwriting coming to life, leaving many people—including me—wondering if there is anything to graphology.

The physical weight of *The Collected Works* (Words?) is striking! As a fellow writer, I immediately thought: *how did he write so much when he was drunk all the time?* The word *prolific* comes to mind, but since so much of the previously unpublished work is presented without much organization, the jury is out on its quality as an oeuvre.

The challenge with most "collected works" tomes is that the collecting part sometimes includes things the artist either specifically did not want published or may have still been editing toward publication. This is not particular to Jim's collection. Researchers have brought out similar books on nearly every writer of note across genres—for instance, Hemingway's lost novels and Fitzgerald's marginalia. What Morrison's collected writings reveal is his sharp insight and ability to create symbols and metaphors, but an intelligence that needed to be harnessed, as if he were reacting to the heaviness of the world in fragments—often brilliant, often needing more time to marinate and coalesce.

Interviews with those who worked with Jim on his self-published poetry books—*The Lords and the New Creatures* (1969) and *An American Prayer* (1970)—reveal that when it came to his writing, he was highly organized and knew precisely how he wanted the book to look and feel. You don't get that sense with *The Collected Works*. The many photos of scenes from his life and notebook pages actually work *against* the readability of the whole. It seems to me that Jim would have wanted the focus to be on the words, not the images.

Ginny Ganahl, the Doors' secretary in 1968 and 1969, worked with Morrison on his poetry books. From her recollection, he viewed them as "his project that he undertook" outside the band. "He knew what he wanted," Ganahl said. When the books finally arrived at the Doors office, he signed a few, then turned to her and exclaimed: "Now I can die happy." She thought it was a lighthearted thought because he was so happy in the moment, though, not as a premonition of early death or a wish to die. "He was an artist and it was a limited edition of his work and I think it meant a lot to him."

In 1988 and 1990, the initial push to recognize Jim for his writing life outside the Doors had launched with the publication of *Wilderness: The Lost Writings of Jim Morrison* and *The American Night: The Writings of Jim Morrison* (1990). Like so many Gen X college students back then, I gobbled up both books, primarily out of curiosity over the clash in my mind between the teenage image I had of Morrison versus the college version. Another great reference from this period is *The Doors: The Complete Illustrated Lyrics*, edited by Danny Sugerman, which provides all the lyrics and some added from live performances, in addition to several essays on the band from when they were active.

The Collected Works was edited by Morrison's friend and unofficial historian Frank Lisciandro. I don't know Frank and although I find the writing collection not what I would have done in terms of format and layout, I would like to convey my deep thanks to him for dedicating so much of his life to keeping *the real* Jim Morrison alive. His collection of interviews, *Jim Morrison: Friends Gathered Together* (2014), is, in my mind, the single most important book that has been published about its subject.

Although some historians and researchers might have a slight criticism with how the questions in the book were asked—Lisciandro seems overly concerned with debunking Morrison's relationship with Patricia Kennealy—the straightforward presentation of Jim by people who spent time with him and knew him personally grows more important each day as the sheer number of those who knew him shrinks. Lisciandro's book is simply stunning in how it reveals who Morrison was and how deeply loved—despite his flaws—he was by his friends. How the thesis shines is embodied in one of Frank's many comments about his friend: "I appreciated his sense of humor, his easygoing manner and his quiet, brilliant mind." This explicit commitment to the authentic Jim revealed in Lisciandro's quote is why the collection of interviews is powerful. The book provides a counterbalance to the many histories and interviews that focus principally on Morrison's drunken behavior without assessing his life and world in proper context.

The secondary literature on the Doors and/or Jim is kind of wildly interesting and overtly disappointing at the same time. Most people who have read a book about Morrison got their initial introduction through Jerry Hopkins and Danny Sugerman in *No One Here Gets Out Alive* (1980). This is the one that I grew up on and, depending on your age, was most likely your first deep dive into the Lizard King. The book is a classic of rock journalism—it more or less launched the behind-the-scenes band/performer history—and continues to be popular based on the Morrison myths it established.

At my high school, and countless others in the Eighties onward, the book was passed among friends and others, a kind of rite of passage if you were a teen boy of a certain age. Now, certainly, that is not an inclusive way of looking at the book, but speaking from experience and in talking to hundreds of other Gen Xers, teenage male readers definitely drove *No*

One Here. The back cover copy is frozen in time, designed to attract that early 1980s reader, announcing: "Here is Jim Morrison in all his complexity—singer, philosopher, poet, delinquent . . . obsessed disciple of darkness. . . ." All the Gen X buzzwords and attention-grabbers, which ultimately set the tone for how Morrison's legend was formed.

If there is a weakness—major or minor, depending on your perspective—*No One Here Gets Out Alive* plays fast and loose with the definition of "nonfiction." There are many scenes, episodes, and quotes that could only have come from Morrison himself and he was dead—despite the *Is he really dead?* rumors that the authors wanted to plant in the nation's collective consciousness. No one who reads *No One* comes out of the exercise without a strong opinion of Jim Morrison—a hedonistic rock god or misguided poet. The criticism of Hopkins and Sugerman increased when *The Doors* film came out because it was leaked that Oliver Stone used it as a primary source for the script and his vision of Jim.

In his book, *Behind Closed Doors*, Hopkins confessed:

Many have credited (blamed?) *No One Here Gets Out Alive*, along with Francis Ford Coppola's artful mix of napalm and "The End" in *Apocalypse Now*, for bringing the Doors back to life. The book has also been nailed for kickstarting the Morrison dead-or-alive myth. I plead partly guilty. Yes, I threw the facts and theories and fantasies surrounding his death into a blender, thereby obscuring the truth. I did so deliberately.

Regardless of how you look at *No One Here*, it has been enormously valuable. Some call it a cult classic, and it certainly has those features. I have my yellowing, pages-falling-out paperback copy here on my desk.

So you are now deep in your Doors/Morrison journey—where else might you look? As I mentioned, the secondary literature is not as robust as one might like, much of it filled with the obsessive overturn-every-garbage-can details that some readers might find interesting, kind of like the crazed work "Dylanologists" have done to dissect every moment of Dylan's long life. So wade in, but do so based on your interest level.

Three older books examine Jim and the band. *Break On Through: The Life and Death of Jim Morrison* by James Riordan and Jerry Prochnicky (1991, 2006) examines Morrison's early life and, alternatively, provides additional insight into his tragic death. Stephen Davis's *Jim Morrison: Life, Death, Legend* (2004) has an agenda—presenting odd theories about the singer that not only turned off Doors fans but are wildly out of tune with the social norms of contemporary readers. *Love Becomes a Funeral Pyre: A Biography of the Doors* by Mick Wall (2015) is a "revisionist" history, attempting to re-center Morrison and his bandmates in contrast to the earlier biographies (along with heavy doses of snark and criticism).

There are other books that an interested reader should examine, including *Angels Dance and Angels Die: The Tragic Romance of Pamela and Jim Morrison* by Patricia Butler, a thorough dual biography of (the original) Jim and Pam. Gillian G. Gaar's *The Doors: The Illustrated History* brings together solid research with a wealth of photos and images that contextualizes the band and its era. *The Doors: A Lifetime of Listening to Five Mean Years* (2011) by Greil Marcus is an interesting book that you will either love or hate. Some people do not get Marcus's style, one that is sometimes ambling and rambling. *The Doors Examined* (2013) by Jim Cherry is a collection of his essays, which includes book reviews and other aspects of the band's history that many readers will find thought-provoking.

There are a handful of memoirs, which you can easily find, including by Patricia Kennealy and other women in Jim's life. Two provides glimpses of Morrison early in his career, including *I'm With the Band: Confessions of a Groupie* by Pamela Des Barres (1987). I recommend the memoir *Love Her Madly: Jim Morrison, Mary, and Me* by Bill Cosgrove (2020), a fascinating view of 1965 and the author's friendship with Jim and his first true love, the mysterious Mary Werbelow. The value of the book is that it gives a portrait of Jim from a part of his life not as fully understood as the rock-star years.

For context on the war in Vietnam, the Sixties and Seventies, and more, take a look at the following (although an exhaustive list could be a book in itself): *The Shattering: America in the 1960s* by Kevin Boyle (2021); *Boomers: The Men and Women Who Promised Freedom and Delivered Disaster* by Helen Andrews (2021); *A Generation of Sociopaths: How the Baby Boomers Betrayed America* by Bruce Cannon Gibney (2017); *Witness to the Revolution: Radicals, Resisters, Vets, Hippies, and the Year America Lost Its Mind and Found Its Soul* by Clara Bingham (2016); *American Empire: The Rise of a Global Power, the Democratic*

Revolution at Home, 1945–2000 by Joshua Freeman (2012); *1968 in America: Music, Politics, Chaos, Counterculture, and the Shaping of a Generation* by Charles Kaiser (1988);

On Vietnam: *Vietnam: An Epic Tragedy, 1945–1975* by Max Hastings (2018); *Enduring Vietnam: An American Generation and Its War* by James Wright (2017); *Kill Anything that Moves: The Real American War in Vietnam* by Nick Turse (2013).

On addiction and psychology: *The Urge: Our History of Addiction* by Carl Erik Fisher (2022); *Drunk: How We Sipped, Danced, and Stumbled Our Way to Civilization* by Edward Slingerland (2021); *Drink?: The New Science of Alcohol and Health* by David Nutt (2020); *The Narcissist You Know: Defending Yourself Against Extreme Narcissists in an All-About-Me Age* by Joseph Burgo (2015).

Of course, a comprehensive bibliography would run into hundreds of pages and include fiction from the era and today, biographies and memoirs of dozens of other rock stars, insiders, and those on the peripheries of these interesting lives. This is just a glimpse into some categories that I studied.

It is not surprising that so many books exist on the Sixties and Seventies era. Perhaps the fascinating idea is that there is still so much more to learn and be written.

ABOUT THE AUTHOR

ob Batchelor is a cultural historian and noted expert on contemporary American culture, history, and biography. His books examine modern popular-culture icons, events, and issues, from comic books and music to literary figures and history's outlaws.

Batchelor has published books on Stan Lee, *The Great Gatsby*, *Mad Men*, and John Updike, among others. *Rookwood: The Rediscovery and Revival of an American Icon, An Illustrated History* won the 2021 Independent Publishers Book Award for Fine Art. *The Bourbon King: The Life and Crimes of George Remus, Prohibition's Evil Genius* won the 2020 Independent Publishers Book Award for Historical Biography. *Stan Lee: The Man Behind Marvel* was a finalist for the 2018 Ohioana Book Award for Nonfiction. His latest book is *Stan Lee: A Life* (2022) and *Stan Lee: The Man Behind Marvel*, Young Adult's Edition (2022).

Batchelor's books have been translated into a dozen languages. His work has appeared or been featured in the *New York Times*, *Cincinnati Enquirer*, *Los Angeles Times*, Today.com, *The Guardian*, and *Time*. Batchelor is a host on the New Books Network podcast and creator and host of the podcast *John Updike: American Writer, American Life*. He has appeared as an on-air commentator for the National Geographic Channel, *PBS NewsHour*, BBC, PBS, and NPR.

Batchelor earned a doctorate in American Literature from the University of South Florida. Bob and his wife Suzette live in North Carolina and have two wonderful teenage daughters. Visit him at www.bobbatchelor.com.

Roadhouse Blues is set in 10-point Sabon, which was designed by the German-born typographer and designer Jan Tschichold (1902–1974) in the period 1964–1967. It was released jointly by the Linotype, Monotype, and Stempel type foundries in 1967. Copyeditor for this project was Shannon LeMay-Finn. The book was designed by Brad Norr Design, Minneapolis, Minnesota, and typeset by New Best-set Typesetters Ltd.

CPSIA information can be obtained
at www.ICGtesting.com
Printed in the USA
JSHW020953091022
31428JS00002B/2